VGM Career Books

New York   Chicago   San Francisco   Lisbon   London   Madrid   Mexico City
Milan   New Delhi   San Juan   Seoul   Singapore   Sydney

The *McGraw·Hill* Companies

Library of Congress Cataloging-in-Publication Data

Gearhart, Susan Wood.
    Opportunities in beauty and modeling careers / by Susan Wood Gearhart.
        p.   cm. — (VGM opportunities series)
    ISBN 0-07-143726-6
        1. Beauty culture—Vocational guidance.   2. Models (Persons)—Vocational
guidance.   I. Title.   II. Series.

    TT958.G35   2004
    646.7′2′02373—dc22   2004005886

1 2 3 4 5 6 7 8 9 0   DOC/DOC   3 2 1 0 9 8 7 6 5 4

ISBN 0-07-143726-6

Interior design by Rattray Design

McGraw-Hill books are available at special quantity discounts to use as premiums and sales promotions, or for use in corporate training programs. For more information, please write to the Director of Special Sales, Professional Publishing, McGraw-Hill, Two Penn Plaza, New York, NY 10121-2298. Or contact your local bookstore.

This book is printed on acid-free paper.

To Marguerite and Wm. Barker Wood,
Gabrielle, Chris, Finn, and Van

CONTENTS

Haircutters. Hair colorists. Manicurists and
pedicurists. Makeup artists. Electrolysis. Research.
Management. Cosmetology instructors. Using
cosmetology education for other careers.
Entrepreneurial cosmetologists.

Public schools. Private schools. Advanced training.
Apprenticeships. Licensing requirements. Sample
cosmetology curricula. Licensing and training nail
technicians. Specialized courses. Limited certificates.
Supplemental courses. Training for instructors.

Foreword

BEAUTY HAS ALWAYS been prized. From the ancients to the Renaissance to the moderns, from poets to artists to common folk, beauty is much admired and much sought after. This holds true today. If there are any doubts, one has only to look through magazines, at billboards, at television; the message is clear. Beauty is worth it.

Perhaps it seems superficial to rely only on one's looks to make it in this world. In fact, this is not true. Today, it takes just as much (if not more) in brains and savvy to earn a living in the beauty industry as it does in any other highly competitive field. You'll put as much time and effort into this career as into any other worthwhile life's work. And you will find satisfaction, not only in the work you as a model will do, but in the work that you as a cosmetologist will do for your clients.

This field offers a wide variety of options. Perhaps you will make it as the next highly paid high fashion model, traveling the globe and enjoying the life this career will make possible for you. Very few of us can reach this pinnacle of success, and even if we do, it's a career that will, of necessity, be short-lived. Happily, the industry offers so much more to those who are attracted to it.

Hair, skin, nails—these are the raw materials you will mold and shape for your clients. Helping people bring out the best in their features brings tremendous satisfaction not only to you, but also to your clients, who leave your care feeling and looking like that million dollars that high fashion models earn.

No matter the path you choose to follow in the world of beauty—model, manicurist, hairstylist, aesthetician, to name just a few—you are sure to enjoy a challenging, yet richly rewarding career.

The Editors, VGM Career Books

Acknowledgments

My GRATITUDE AND appreciation are extended to the following people for their kindness, help, and time. Among those to whom I want to express special thanks are: Joel Kutun, B.A., CLS, electrologist and laser specialist, Long Island, New York; Mary Looram, TV commercials model, New York City; Joe Tristino, owner/manager of Linea Day Spa Salon, Glen Ellyn, Illinois; Diane Barron and Kathy Triche, DSW, for their endless help and encouragement; Andre Mitchell for his computer help; Daniela Guggenheim, for her tireless and wonderful professional assistance; Nancy Joseffer, for her kind support and thoughtfulness; Lea Diluca, for her inspiring inner and outer beauty; Gabrielle Conley, for her daily loving support and research; Barbara Donner, former editor, NTC Publishing Group; Finn Conley, for his exuberant enthusiasm and loving patience; and Fergus, for his majestic bearing and affection.

Careers in Today's Beauty Industry

Naturally we want to look the best we can. Many people believe that what they look like is a reflection of the care they put into their jobs and personal lives. Consequently they pursue the people, products, and services that will help them put their best faces forward. This translates into numerous job opportunities in the beauty profession. Here are some of the more lucrative careers you might consider.

Haircutters

"Your crowning glory is your greatest asset" is a very old adage. Today more than ever, a good haircut defines that glory. Hairdressers all must strive to create a basic cut that the client can work with when he or she walks out of the salon. This takes awareness of different hair textures and how they are affected by the elements, chemicals, age, and climate. Hair is a difficult medium to work with, and your basic training starts you on your way to understanding what implements work best. Hair slides from the scissors, exhibits ragged edges, and sticks out at odd angles. You can see just how crucial your haircut is when you try to do it yourself.

We are all reliant on the capable professional because hair constantly grows and changes its shape. As hair frames the face, it either enhances your face tremendously or detracts from it. Styles change frequently and often dramatically. Some folks never follow the trend but prefer to keep an old style forever. As the hairdresser, you'll have to render whatever the client demands. A patron often arrives with a magazine photo and expects the same cut. The transfer from idea to reality will be one of your tasks.

Hair in the Western world is very much how we define ourselves. Even our theatrical productions portray how we feel about hair. Shows and movies like *Hair*, *Shampoo*, *Hairspray*, and *Steel Magnolias*, and the classics *Georgie Girl* and *Grease* have plots based on our singularly obsessive hair culture. Celebrities are recognized by their haircuts and ever-changing styles and colors.

We demand that our hairstylist render our wishes, and expediently as well. As a result the indispensability of this quality service, in some cases, has caused the salaries of hairdressers to rise astronomically. In New York City there are several haircutters who command $400 per cut! Few of us can afford their services, but it shows just how valuable the great haircut can be. Often these hairstylists become celebrities themselves and are associated with the famous people and the images they've created. A hairstylist's career can catch a streaking star and rise right along with the newly coiffed personage. These are the truly creative artists of the hairdressing world. Their master classes alone bring in thousands of dollars for an hour of their expertise.

Regardless of your desire to rise to great acclaim, you will be invaluable to your client following and will find satisfaction in a hairstyling career. Creating a becoming haircut for each individual is a rewarding challenge.

Hair Colorists

The most popular hair color in North America is blond, and though some of us started with that coveted hue, few of us keep it for a lifetime. Oxidation and age cause the hair to darken. Movie stars and rock celebrities have set our preferences. They love the way the light-attracting shades give greater notice. Past actors and actresses can still be conjured up in our imaginations due to their famous tresses alone. No talent required. Those who are too young to remember Jean Harlow and Marilyn Monroe still know them as "Blonde Bombshells," as though the color of their hair alone endowed them with desirability and glamour.

Hair color can be temporary or permanent, brash or subtle, shocking or mousey. The greatest colorists are capable of magically creating just the perfect tones. The hair softly shines with the variegated colors. These are the most costly effects to conjure as the expertise of the colorist comes from years of experience. Thus the colorist commands the highest salary in the salon. If you can successfully predict the outcome of the dyes when they are mixed, you will be a very successful colorist. For when a client demands one shade, she or he assumes that you can immediately produce the same. Variations on the theme are not usually embraced with enthusiasm.

In the large cities, bright shades of magenta and scarlet are among the current vibrant preferences for the avant garde. The übermodels have given hair colorists myriads of new challenges.

Photography as well as runway lights can reduce the depth of the desired colors. Companies that produce the rinses and dyes and bleaches have hustled to meet the demand.

The domain of the colorist must encompass everything from the most brilliant shades to the most delicate tints. It's the most challenging area of hairdressing and the most fun as well. Trendsetting is what it's all about. You are creating sophisticated and chic heads. Like the haircutter, the colorist is indispensable to your personal "look." A highly paid professional, the hair colorist can and does rise to that stellar position of celebrity. The processes that go into a perfected head of artificial coloring can be very lengthy and exacting. Several hours are needed to ensure the right outcome. Thousands are spent annually by one client alone for even the most simple of the many processes available.

Manicurists and Pedicurists

The huge difference that well-groomed hands can make is underestimated. Your hands can reflect a sense of cleanliness and grooming that silently tells a lot about you. Even as a small child, I noticed dirty and unkempt nails. Cuticles need care as well as the nail itself, which should be kept to a workable length. All ten nails should match in shape and be appropriate to your lifestyle. Men as well as women need the services of the professional manicurist.

Both manicurists and pedicurists remain seated during their work, unlike hairstylists who must stand all day. At one time the nail technician serviced women who desired a fashion statement with long and brightly colored nails, and today it has once again become a grooming enhancement for both sexes of all ages. The pedicure also is returning to favor as a hygienic rather than strictly cosmetic procedure. So you see more men taking advantage of this service as well.

The nail technician can do very well financially. The procedures are varied and as a result can be moderate to extremely luxurious. Repeat clients are your bread and butter. Most professional businesspeople have a weekly manicure, and that means a nice salary as well as tips. The recent inclusion of leg and arm massages has increased the appeal of these once rather mechanical services.

For the nail technician, the study program is a fairly short one, and for a few weeks of your time as a student you will have a profession that you can use full-time, part-time, and for a lifetime. You are trained to care for the correct growth of the nails on both hands and feet. It is critical that the toenail be groomed for proper placement of the foot inside the shoe. Ingrown nails can be painful as well as dangerous. One needs only to observe the malformed toes and nails at the beach or gym to be aware of how most persons could benefit from the services of a good pedicurist.

Most women like the well-being a manicure/pedicure provides, but they also appreciate the cosmetic enhancement as well. Painting nails is fun and it pulls together the individual's fashion statement. Airbrushing has become the most recent trend for nails. The process can result in a look that is from understated to quite eye-catching. The personal taste of each patron makes this a creative challenge for the technician. There are thousands who have caught the fancy-nail craze. Girls as young as six have come to nail salons to get a fashionable look way ahead of their years. The rise of hundreds of nail salons in every large city tells you that their popularity is still very much a growing thing.

You will notice after several trips to the manicurist that the routine is a very exacting one. A professional manicurist trains the nail to grow in a certain manner to strengthen it and to make the nail more attractive to the eye. The end of the nail can be treated so that breakage is kept to a minimum.

Makeup Artists

The enormous popularity of the complete-makeover television shows has given rise to a new revered status for makeup artists. They are key to turning a tired or insipid face into a vibrant and more youthful look. One needs only to observe the drastic change in the makeup of newscasters to be aware of the importance of the new look. The ladies who relay the daily news now appear as if they are ready to step out of the studio into a party. Smooth, flawless skin can be created by the brushes and the artistic eye of these magicians. I was recently mesmerized by the transformation of an already very attractive talk-show hostess into an absolutely glowing golden appearance. She is a big proponent of the makeover and has single-handedly made the public aware of the artistry of makeup.

The makeup artist learns his or her trade one face at a time. Many products are used on each face, but it is how they are combined that creates the final portrait. A trace amount of multiple textures and hues is required, and the wizardry of the makeup artist is well renowned. Balance is everything. Like the hair colorist, you will have to develop visual acuity and comprehend mixes with subtle yet different tones. In bygone days, the fair of face really had little competition, but today, the makeup artist is enhancing those less fortunate faces with corrective color, shading, and thus new presentability.

The pay scale for the aesthetician is notoriously high. This is the luxury end of the cosmetology world. Everyone needs to have their hair groomed and some, perhaps because of their jobs, are forced to keep coloring it to present a younger image. But professionally applied makeup is prohibitively expensive and thus remains an extremely high-salaried position. Lavish weddings, modeling shows, movies, and video productions hire the makeup artist. The locations are always changing, unless you work for a makeup company, and even then you are often moved from store to store. The very finest makeup artist hired by the cosmetic company could land a position in a high-end boutique, where you would find yourself applying your artistry to clients who are expected to make serious purchases from the myriad of products used.

As Americans, we are starting to become aware of facial treatments to keep our skin younger and healthier. We used to be consumed with the idea of makeup only, but the preparation of the skin itself has become very much a part of the aesthetician's goal. Facial treatments also are quite expensive, so if you should decide to enter this area of cosmetology, your salary would be quite high. Some cosmeticians combine the two services and will do the preliminary cleansing to prepare the face and then apply the makeup to complete the procedure. It would depend on the size of the salon where you would be employed as to the feasibility of such a position. The cost of facial treatments is, unfortunately, prohibitive for the mainstream to take advantage of. So if you opt to work in this category, you are quite well guaranteed of luxurious surroundings and of a compensatory salary. Most women and men who avail themselves of facial treatments and massages do so on a rather sporadic schedule, say once a month.

Makeup artists can enhance your color, hide scars and discolorations, give you expressive eyes, correct imbalances through illusions created, and transform you into an unrecognizable being. This end of aesthetics is the fashion arena of ever-changing looks. The creative challenge is always present. Makeup artists are so highly paid for their skilled work that they are hired per hour rather than per day. The best areas with the highest demand for really great makeup artists are New York City and Los Angeles.

Being a makeup artist means that you will have to be a trend-setter, as the world of cosmetics at that level is always desirous of the "new" and more daring. Sometimes the person being made up needs to look very old, sick, ghoulish, angelic, innocent, romantic, or weathered. Your job would be the challenge of any or all of these effects manifested through pencils, brushes, and colors.

Electrolysis

Electrolysis is one of several types of processes that permanently remove the hair from the body. It is a somewhat tedious procedure for both the operator and the client as so few hairs can be removed in one session. The biggest competition to the electrologist is the laser removal technique. In some states the medical doctor is the operator for laser, and in other states the cosmetologist is able to do laser treatment.

Excessive hair is a serious problem for those who suffer from hir-sutism, and you will be doing a much appreciated service in getting rid of unwanted body hair. Our society sets standards as to what is aesthetically acceptable. So if one is plagued with facial hair that is not easily disguised, the consequences can be terribly embarrassing. There is a bit of discomfort in the electrology procedure, and as a result the patron must usually make several visits to accomplish the complete removal of all the unwanted hair. Each hair follicle must be separately dealt with, which causes the procedure to be quite expensive. You will do very well as an electrologist if you are patient, reassuring, and gentle. There can be negative repercussions if you are not careful. Scarring and burns have resulted from improper administration of electrolysis. Therefore, you must carry insurance that will protect you if something should go wrong while you are working on a patron. Many of your clients will have special desires to be hair-free, and your expertise in all types and areas of body hair will be required if you want to be successful. Your clients are having permanent hair removal, which means they are not repeat customers, but you hope that they will be so pleased with your services that they will recommend you to others.

Research

The never-ending formulations of new cosmetic products are done in laboratories. Their creation involves the product as well as elaborate testing. I was recently paid to participate in a three-month-long study to test the effectiveness of a new cream. We were photographed before and after. This live study is fairly typical of laboratory research. There is much challenging work for those interested in this end of cosmetology. Many years of experience in the beauty world and a college degree in chemistry are the prerequisites for this position. You would be responsible for the careful preparation of the newly formed cosmetic products and formulas. Possible allergic reactions and adverse reactions have to be ruled out before a product can be marketed. The reputation of the cosmetic company is at stake, to say nothing of endless lawsuits in our litigious society.

This is a highly paid job, as your position is key to the high standards maintained as well as the creation of competitive emollients in the cosmetic industry. Billions of dollars are spent by those who hope these products will actually deliver the results they promise.

Management

Many cosmetologists desire to be their own boss. As such they open a beauty salon, barbershop, day spa, or school, or they opt to manage a franchise. Your knowledge as a cosmetologist gives you needed insight to have a successful business.

If you wish to advance in a managerial position, you will need to be diplomatic, a wise employer, an efficient scheduler for employees and clients, and well organized. You will have to be aware of your state's laws regarding sanitation, special regulations, procedures, and licenses needed. Equipment must be kept up to standard and you will need good judgment to keep competitive. Beauty establishments are particularly prone to the fickle whims of a bevy of clients.

Cosmetology Instructors

Do you enjoy sharing your knowledge and are you blessed with patience? To be a good instructor, you will need to be dedicated to your students and their various needs. Your employment could be in a vocational or a private beauty school. If you select a specialty, you could travel to dozens of schools demonstrating specific skills.

There are many positions available in teaching, so do your research while you are still a student yourself. Be aware of your instructors' capabilities and shortcomings so that you will be a better teacher. One famous hairstylist has a handpicked few who travel around the world to give lessons on how to cut in his signature manner. This instructor guides well-trained technicians through the exacting methods. Each student is working on a live model and as such acquires a genuine understanding of the procedures.

Using Cosmetology Education for Other Careers

Necessity is the mother of invention and thousands of beauty products are thus created annually. A newly released balm addresses the desire to reduce the visibility of facial scars. Wider ranges of cosmetic colors are created for ethnic needs. Longer-lasting formulas are desired as we face time limitations in our busy lives. We are also seeing an overlap in medical and cosmetic products. With the advent of so much facial surgery, we are now employing special cosmeticians to bridge the gap. Postsurgery salves now do double duty—part healing and part cover-up.

Cosmetic sales positions are an entirely separate thing, and you may want to be a licensed cosmetologist to present the product more efficiently. In most states you would be forbidden to touch your patron without that license. A virtual gold mine is awaiting a super sales representative. Is there a celebrity out there who hasn't taken advantage of endorsing his or her own signature line? There are many sales positions awaiting the expertise of an energetic cosmetician.

Perhaps you enjoy writing and wish to combine your cosmetological wisdom with your creative ability in that area. Your talents could be incorporated in a myriad of ways, from the instructions on the product to a beauty column in a magazine. Beauty is an enormous business, and you could potentially write for TV shows, lectures, advertisement copy, or even books. You can make a niche with your special knowledge and expand it.

Entrepreneurial Cosmetologists

With the advent of the Internet, we see endless opportunities for entrepreneurs. The Web is an ideal arena for cosmetologists to ply their services and wares. The reachable public is limitless. Everything from the makeup artist to the medically oriented cosmetic manipulation is displayed for consumers.

On a more personal level, an entrepreneur may wish to open a day spa. Unlike the beauty salon, all services are available under one roof in the day spa. Where it used to be service oriented, it now is a "spa" in as much as clients leave feeling rejuvenated as well as completely groomed. Time is always of the essence, and in the past the many grooming procedures were accomplished effectively. Now they are accomplished with panache as well. These services come with a very high price tag, but they are accommodating to one's specific needs and can be had at odd hours and on days like Sunday.

2

Educational and Licensing Requirements for the Beauty Industry

THERE ARE MANY options open to you as you begin to research your educational needs in the cosmetology industry. This chapter will help guide you to the best path to follow given your particular interests and abilities.

Public Schools

If you can locate an approved public cosmetology school you will be able to save both time and money. Taking courses at a public school during your high school years is a way to avoid the normal beauty school costs. The high school curriculum starts when you are in the eleventh grade for three hours a day. In the summer, you take training for six hours a day, and you will take three hours a day of courses during the twelfth grade. In vocational centers and community colleges, classroom time varies. If a student has completed all required subjects, he or she will attend classes for five to six hours each day. Postsecondary training is taught at a rate of five to six hours each day, with entire courses taking anywhere from six hundred to twelve hundred hours, as required by law. Individual schools must certify that students are ready for the exams.

Many public schools in California offer cosmetology courses. A list of these qualified establishments may be obtained by e-mailing or writing to the California State Board of Cosmetology in care of the California Department of Consumer Affairs. Its Web address is dea.ca.gov/barber. Part-time attendance at a school of cosmetology will meet California's law requirements that all students must attend a public school until their eighteenth birthday. After a person reaches that age, he or she can take cosmetology courses full-time, and then be licensed.

Certain states like Florida have an extensive system of public cosmetology schools located in high schools, education centers, vocational centers, junior colleges, community colleges, adult programs, and adult centers. These technical facilities are scattered all over the state so they are readily reached.

Other states offer comprehensive cosmetology programs in their public school system. The junior year in high school seems the normal time to start these classes. If you are interested in taking cosmetology courses while you are still in high school and your school doesn't offer that curriculum, try to locate another school in your area where you can take advantage of this public instruction.

Accreditation is controlled at the state level; thus you must pass an examination that is recognized only by that one state. State cosmetology boards see to the regulations of schools, businesses, and licensing. There has been a movement for decades to federalize these examinations, with no real solution. There is limited reciprocity, though, among some states, but you may be required to take additional courses, put in more hours, or merely take the other state's exam. Be sure to write, e-mail, or call the state board of cosmetology where you plan to attend beauty school and get answers to your questions. Know the legal aspects of that particular state so as not to make costly mistakes in your choices of curriculum. All states stress different areas of cosmetological studies. If you know what you need to practice in a certain state, you can make wiser decisions.

It would be impossible to list every beauty school or to point out every advantage of getting your cosmetology education at one school or another. But we will try to cover several types of cosmetology educational offerings located in several states to give you an idea of what is generally available.

Beauty courses break down into three categories: public, private, and advanced training schools.

There are more than 80 approved public cosmetology schools in Florida, if both day and evening schools are taken into consideration. California's many public cosmetology schools can be located in junior colleges, occupational centers, and adult learning centers.

Some schools, strictly speaking, are neither public nor private. You will pay a small amount of money for your education, but because of state funds within that particular school, your tuition will be much less than it would be at a private beauty school. These are considerations that you will want to take into account before you decide upon a school.

Private Schools

There are extensive differences in some of the private cosmetology schools due to instructors, standards of education required of the instructor, and the attitude and ability of the manager of the school. Make certain that the school you select is properly accredited by contacting that state's cosmetology board. One young student revealed her technique for locating the best school for her. She suggested going to the best salons in town and asking their newest operators and apprentices where they took their basic training. One way of judging the quality of a school's curriculum is to find out whether that school's graduates are getting jobs after graduation. After all, that is your primary concern. You may already know that a particular salon is your choice for work, so don't be shy about talking to its manager and finding out his or her preferences in cosmetology graduates. He or she will be glad to tell you. The manager is running a successful business and intends to keep up its standards by hiring well-instructed graduates.

Advanced Training

Advanced training in cosmetology is offered to further your current knowledge. This curriculum is mentioned only briefly, as you may or may not elect to attend advanced training. In certain beauty salons new methods are shown to operators so that they can incorporate the current styles or trends that have just come into fashion. Fashion is constantly changing, and makeup and hairstyles must keep up with the latest look. If you are an operator whose patrons demand the latest haircuts, coloring, and styles, and your salon does not provide a periodic demonstrator, you will want to attend master classes to learn some fine points. In these classes, you will benefit from the experience and wisdom of a well-established professional hairstylist. It may be someone known as a competition hair designer, a precision cutter, or a recognized colorist. Any added knowledge that you acquire will surely mean added clients and, of course, the compensatory salary and tips. These special schools may appear to be extremely expensive, but the $100 or more you pay for the class could mean a sizeable increase in your income.

Apprenticeships

After you have completed your state licensing, you may want to apprentice in a better salon. This would help you to develop as a capable hairstylist and earn a better salary. If you desire to be associated with a salon with a reputation for high style or trendsetting, you must be prepared to accept very low compensation while you closely observe a well-established operator in that particular salon. You will be expected to put in normal working hours (usually an eight-hour day) and do everything that is asked of you by the busy top hairstylists. This could include shampooing, assisting with hair treatments, holding hair clips, and drying hair. You will not do haircutting or final styling until you have learned all the fine points of the specialized techniques. You could apprentice for as many as two to three years in a very elaborate salon. It all depends on your ability to learn to cut hair with dexterity and cleverness. There are specific haircuts and styles that better-known salons have made famous. To learn a detailed type of cut is painstaking but absolutely necessary.

Apprentices Prior to Certification

Certain states have regulations that prohibit students from apprenticing before securing a license. An apprentice is someone who learns by on-the-job training. The difference in this type of apprenticeship from the type just discussed is that this apprentice is clearly a trainee and has not yet accumulated the required educational hours to take the state boards. In some states where apprentices are schooled in beauty salons, state regulations will designate in every detail the registration requirements for the apprentice and the instructor-to-apprentice ratio in the place of business. In states that permit apprentices, strict laws stipulate all the conditions under which apprentices may be trained. These laws are clearly stated in the brochures put out by the specific state. If you are considering training as an apprentice prior to taking your state boards, it is imperative that you read all materials pertinent to registered apprentices. The fee paid by apprentices is not listed in most advertising brochures. Also, be sure to make inquiries at your local beauty salon to see where you actually would take all the needed courses. They may or may not be given in the same location.

Apprenticeships vary in actual required hours from state to state. The average appears to be two years of noncertified, but registered, apprenticeship in a beauty salon under the tutelage of the designated number of certified operators. The required years of work would differ according to the individual's capabilities.

Licensing Requirements

Before you make plans to enroll in any cosmetology course, be sure to find out the minimum age at which you can get a license. Some states don't even permit the state examinations until a particular age, so determine when you will be able to take the exam before you enroll. The minimum age and amount of formal education required for licensure differs from state to state. The average age for entry into cosmetology schools seems to be 16. Average schooling requirements vary much more widely. In Texas, for example, you can enroll in cosmetology school at the age of 16, and you need only have completed the seventh grade in elementary school. In

Washington, D.C., you need only to have completed the eighth grade, but must be 16 years old. So you can see that there is a variance in licensing requirements among the states.

Some states allow special testing for people who do not speak English well. If English is not your first language, investigate your state laws through a translator. Many states provide a practical test rather than a written test for those who do not speak English.

Application for Licensure

When you have completed the required number of school hours for your state, you must apply to take the state board examinations. Your state has forms that are prescribed by the state cosmetology board. Every state has different time schedules to be followed, and you should check to see how far in advance you need to apply to take the exams at the designated time. You may find that application has to be made weeks or months in advance. So even if you have not yet graduated from beauty school, look into scheduling your exam.

There is also a fee, called the initial licensing fee, that must be paid to the state when you take your state boards. You will want to set that amount aside ahead of time.

When the time comes to actually obtain your license, inquire about renewal procedures. Your license is not a lifetime affair. It has to be renewed once every year in some states and once every two years in others. Most states have a set month wherein you are to renew cosmetology licenses. In New York, for instance, cosmetology licenses are renewed on July 1. Check with your state and any other where you may want to work in the future to learn about procedures. Because of large amounts of paperwork, state departments are always very slow, so licensing takes time. Be sure that you have proper licensing so that waiting to receive a license does not cost you working days.

Reciprocity between states means that if you are a licensed operator in one state, your training is recognized by many other states with similar cosmetology licensing rules and regulations. Wherever required hours and courses are alike, you probably will be able to attain a temporary license from the new state until you acquire a permanent license. Again, time will be of the essence. State departments are not intentionally trying to slow you down or prevent you from working, but you should allow several months in most states to receive all the necessary documents after you have made your initial application.

Licensing Examination

There is a National Cosmetology Examination now offered in 32 states. This test, consisting of 100 questions, can be as long as one and a half hours or as short as one hour. Records of the test are kept in the National Interstate Council of State Boards of Cosmetology.

There are special books now in print or on the Internet that will help you study to pass either the regular state boards in your state or the national examination. The books will help you to know what to expect in the exams and how to conduct yourself at the examination. They also give you sample questions to test your knowledge in all the areas that you are expected to understand. When you know what to expect and what types of questions will be asked, you will be much better prepared and less worried about either the written or the practical tests.

Ask at your local bookstore for the books; if they are not in stock, the bookstore can order them for you so you can brush up on all the work that you have covered in your cosmetology courses.

Sample Cosmetology Curricula

Many state-approved cosmetology courses are very similar. Approximately 1,600 hours are expected from the student who wishes to become a licensed practitioner. Each of us learns at a different pace. So if you are patient and listen carefully, your learning experience will be greatly enhanced. Your curriculum is broken down into lectures and demonstrations; you will learn what to do and then you will learn by doing. Your work is of a very serious nature as you will be working with potentially dangerous implements and solutions. In the beginning you will learn all the regulations of cosmetology and barbering. These are important for your entire time spent in the beauty industry. It is comparable to learning to drive a car. There is a correct procedure for each process, and you will be taught the most efficient method in beauty school.

State regulators oversee all regulations. You will learn about the physical composition of hair, nails, and skin and how they need to be cared for hygienically. Products that affect the anatomy and how they work together chemically will be demonstrated. You will see how caustic or toxic solutions must be handled to protect both yourself and the patron. Safety is also a concern in the manipulations of electrical and manually used instruments. Scissors, nippers, dryers, and razors all present individual potential dangers.

Sanitation is crucial as you are touching many people. The physical contact could cause a communicable disease to be transmitted if you are not careful. Fungal infections, viruses, and HIV/AIDS are just a few of these threats. Sanitizing is accomplished through electrical as well as solution methods. It only takes one fungal infection to have clients shun your beauty salon.

The part that you've probably been waiting for will arrive with haircutting and styling classes. These are the services most used by clients and therefore are the recipients of the longest amount of time in the curriculum. You will be instructed how to place rollers, use the scissors correctly, and get the hair to respond to certain patterns. Creativity is a long way away. It will take many years after your graduation before you reach mastery in the hairstyling arena. You have the power through your abilities to fulfill dreams and to create a good self-image for your clients. There is a right way and a wrong way to handle your client, and remember that you will be tipped accordingly.

The finer aspects of facials, eyebrow arching, and depilatories will be taught. After you have completed all the various courses, you will have an idea as to what area you enjoyed most. This will dictate whether you wish to further your education or seek work immediately.

Manicures and pedicures are two more procedures that you will be introduced to in beauty school. The hygienic values as well as the cosmetic artifice are demonstrated and overseen as you try these operations on your fellow students. Another interesting part of cosmetology school is the opportunity to do procedures on the public. These patrons allow for the fact that you are still a student and pay accordingly, but they afford you the exposure to the real future client.

Some schools actually teach psychology courses wherein you learn to deal with the many personalities that will certainly come your way when you are involved with the public.

As you investigate your options in attending cosmetology schools, be aware of the slight differences in curriculum and use them to your advantage. If a school doesn't cover chemical peels and your goal is to be an aesthetician, look for a different cosmetology institute.

This beauty school curriculum comes from a catalog advertisement of a private cosmetology establishment located in New York

City. The classes represent what you could expect to learn if you went there. The cost is approximately $10,000 for 1,000 hours.

Course	Total Hours
1. Finger-Waving	200
2. Permanent Waving	175
3. Haircutting and Hairstyling	125
4. Dyes, Bleaches, and Rinses	100
5. Scalp Treatment	50
6. Shampoos	25
7. Manicuring	100
8. Facials	50
9. Sanitation, Sterilization, Hygiene, and Anatomy	50
10. Tests and Exams	25
11. Shop Management and Business Ethics	50
12. Nondesignated Time	50
Total	1,000

After the completion of the diversified courses in the cosmetology curriculum, you may find yourself doing any or all of the various jobs in a beauty salon. Or you may want to specialize.

Licensing and Training Nail Technicians

New laws and positions have come about due to the extremely rapid growth of this industry. Maine, for example, has a manicurist apprentice license available that requires the operator-in-training to be under the direct supervision of a licensed individual in a licensed shop. In most states a set number of school hours must be taken to qualify for the nail technician's license. The hours vary from 100 to 500 hours, depending on the state. These lessons are to be taken in a licensed cosmetology or licensed nail school. The cost for this schooling varies from school to school but runs generally from $995 to $1,400.

The manicurist manager's license is offered in several states. This position would entail authorizing only cosmetic care of nails. Requirements vary from 100 to 300 hours of schooling beyond the manicurist's license to fulfill this position. The tuition ranges from $370 to $2,000, depending upon the particular school.

The nail technician instructor could be employed in either a nail school or a cosmetology school. This specialty has grown so rapidly over the past few years that the demand for manicurists alone without hairdressing skills has created a vast market in itself. A nail technician instructor fills this post by having been a licensed nail technician first and then completing instructor training, which is about 350 to 1,000 hours of schooling. Tuition for the course is approximately $4,500 for the 1,000 hours. A salary of about $800 to $1,000 per week would be the expected wage for the position in and around New York City.

The nail salon manager, or for that matter any person with a license in manicuring, could well own his or her own nail salon. These can be extraordinarily successful as there is minimal expense for equipment. A few manicure tables and a small, clean, and well-lighted salon are the basic requirements. Your operators usually take home half of their fees plus their tips. You would have half of all the income and any monies you yourself made doing manicures as well. Nail salons are one of the best examples of ultra-successful small businesses. It would be difficult to find an urban city block that doesn't have either a beauty or a nail salon.

Along with the incredible growth of the industry came the discovery that infections can be easily spread from one client to another by using the same implements on many customers. Cut cuticles are an easy source of entry for these infections, and recuperation can take many months. At times, lawsuits have resulted. State health boards took a closer look at the nail industry, and in several states emery boards, chamois buffers, credo knives, and pumice stones are either prohibited or must be used on one patron only. Under the new laws, the manicurists are to be fined for noncompliance if disinfecting machines and antiseptics are not up to the new standards.

Specialized Courses

If you hold a specialty certificate, you are permitted to work in only one particular field. The following definitions of specialties were taken from the General Rules and Regulations, including the Cosmetology Commission Sanitary Rulings from the Texas Cosmetology Commission:

- **Cosmetologist.** A cosmetologist (operator) license authorizes the holder to practice all phases of cosmetology in a beauty salon or any specialties in a specialty shop.
- **Wig specialist.** A wig specialist certificate authorizes the holder to practice wiggery, hair weaving, or perform eye tabbing in a beauty or specialty salon.
- **Manicurist.** A person holding a manicurist license may perform for compensation only the practices of manicuring and pedicuring in a licensed beauty or specialty salon.
- **Shampoo conditioning specialist.** A shampoo specialist certificate authorizes the holder to practice the art of shampooing, application of conditioners and rinses, scalp manipulation, and to sell shampooing hair goods in a licensed beauty or specialty salon.

- **Facial specialist.** A facial specialist certificate authorizes the holder to practice facials, application of facial cosmetics, manipulations, eye tabbing, arches, lash and brow tints, and the temporary removal of facial hair in a licensed beauty or specialty salon.
- **Hair-weaving specialist.** A hair-weaving specialist certificate authorizes the holder to practice the art of hair weaving in a licensed beauty or specialty salon.

The choices for specialization are many. As you can see from the certifications, you might be able to go directly into a special field with only a set curriculum for your specialty area. Or you may have to complete all the required hours in your state, take your state boards, and then specialize. In states with specialty certificates, you cannot perform activities not designated by law. To do so might cause you to have your license revoked. Not all states allow specialty certification courses, but most states do have manicuring-only classes for certification.

Limited Certificates

In some states, you will discover that the license is called a limited certificate. A limited certificate is one that takes only a few school hours to complete. For example, anywhere between 100 and 300 hours could qualify you for a manicurist certificate. A proportionate number of hours are designated to teach you all you need to know on that one topic.

Limited course offerings in cosmetology schools can qualify you to take the state boards in that one special field. Here is a school description of a manicurist course:

Course	Total Hours
1. Orientation	4
2. Manicure Tools and Use	9
3. Nail Structure (Theory)	1
4. Sterilization and Sanitation	2
5. Manicuring Procedure and Hand Massage	84
6. Manicuring Practices	7
7. Manicuring for Men	3
8. Tests	3
Total	113

Some states have no license requirement for manicurists, wig stylists, or assistant manager positions. However, wherever there is a potential health threat, the law is likely to change. You might find yourself having to pick up courses and subsequent licensing.

Supplemental Courses

Being human, we are all subject to changing our minds, and the cosmetological courses of study are now ready to deal with such situations with equanimity. If you find that you are unhappy in your current area of cosmetology, there are solutions that don't require starting from scratch.

A good example of a supplemental curriculum is the cosmetology crossover course for barbers. It consists of 400 hours of technical instruction and practical operations. It would encompass demonstration and lecture and hands-on work with live or stationary mannequins. Nail, hair, and skin care (not already taken in barbering courses) would be taught. Safety precautions like electrical hazards, caustic solutions, and general sanitation to prevent communicable disease would be covered. Hairstyling and coloring by various methods would take up the greatest amount of the crossover courses. There would be about 60 hours devoted to technical lecture and demonstration and 120 hours of actually trying out the newly learned procedures. Both thermal and wet styling, permanent waving, and chemical straightening would be covered. Bleaching of the hair is an often-needed process, and scalp treatment is taught as well. Chemicals associated with facials, peels, scrubs, and dermabrasion are given several hours of concentration. Depilatory methods include tweezers, wax, electrical, and cream. There would be classes in manicuring, pedicuring, makeup, and even eyelash application. At the completion of the required hours, the barber would be ready, legally, to do much more versatile work as well as be more in demand. Fees could very likely triple. The barber is now able to accomplish multiple cosmetic services.

Not every state has this type of arrangement, but it is a great convenience if it exists. This particular crossover course is available in California.

Training for Instructors

Teaching is another area of specialization. There are many positions open to instructors, demonstrators, and even lecturers in the cosmetology field. Some states require special education courses for these posts; others demand only a license in cosmetology from that state and several years of experience as a practical cosmetician. If you are interested in a teaching job, the best way to find out the details is to write or e-mail your state's board of education and find out the current prerequisites. The department can also supply you with the list of all public and private schools of cosmetology where you will be qualified to instruct. Be sure to find out when your license expires and keep it up-to-date. You need to hold a cosmetology license to teach. If you find that your license has expired, you could waste a great deal of time getting it back again. Teacher training varies in hours needed from 600 to 1,000 hours at a cost of between $2,500 and $4,500.

3

WORKING IN BEAUTY SALONS

BEAUTY SALONS PROVIDE the grooming services the public at large seeks. But they can also be categorized by the specific wants and needs of particular clients. This means that you, too, can choose the kind of environment you would like to work in.

Choosing a Place to Work

When you seek employment as a cosmetologist, look in the most desirable spot for you, be it financial, aesthetic, or convenience. Your cosmetology placement service can help you decide where to apply and will guide you toward all feasible openings. There is no crystal ball, so it's up to you to try to foresee your potential for success with patrons, both as you begin your job and after you have been there for a while. It would be unwise to take a position in an area where you know that a competitor at a more desirable location will be opening soon.

Try e-mailing the beauty salons, hotels, department stores, or specialty shops where you think you might like to work. Set up appointments for interviews, and be sure to look neat and well groomed when you go to the interview.

Beauty Shops

Cosmetology jobs are most frequently found in beauty salons. Salons can be situated anywhere, from the local shopping mall to elegant specialty shops. There are many jobs for general operators and specialists alike. The general employment rate in cosmetology is at a healthy 10 percent increase annually. There is tremendous demand for all services, and salons are even more available in suburban areas than ever before. So scout your potential area for possible job availability, and allow for time to find a good position. To have the job you desire, you may have to commute a little. Not all cosmetologists are working, or even desire to do so. Statistics are based both on how many cosmetologists are licensed in a particular state and on how many currently are employed in that state. There are always jobs available in service careers, and cosmetology, in particular, is expanding rapidly in certain high-income areas such as New York, Los Angeles, San Francisco, Atlanta, and Chicago. Finding employment can be more difficult in areas of lower incomes.

Day Spas

Day spas are rapidly becoming extremely popular in large cities due to their ability to provide full cosmetological services all under one roof and in quick and yet luxurious ways. You could have a manicure, pedicure, facial, and a massage all at the same time. This doesn't appeal to everyone, but the day spa has become the choice of the short-of-time woman, be she executive, mother, or homemaker. Time is so limited that all of her beauty needs must be met in perhaps an hour. The availability of many specialists to work simultaneously eliminates her need to run from salon to salon for leg waxing, electrolysis, nail extensions, haircut, styling, dying, and massage. One salon in New York City did all of these services many years ago exclusively for the rich and the famous. So this is not a new idea, but it is certainly a timely one. There are several day spas around, and the advantage for the operators is that they can service many clients in the same amount of time that they would have luxuriously seen only one. Not everyone likes to work in a hurry, so if speediness appeals to you, this could be a good area for investigation. Some clients who avail themselves of day spas are not pressed for time, but many are, and you would be expected to accommodate the patron's specific needs.

Children's Salons

This is a rapidly growing area of the cosmetology world. There are many positions open for shampooing and cutting children's hair. Many malls have special shops to cut children's hair in surroundings oriented to their particular needs. In working with children, patience is a must. Many children wiggle and fuss while having their hair cut. Even if you try everything to calm and distract the child, from bribes of balloons to lollipops, it can still be a challenge. Thankfully, videos are now available and they sometimes hold the youngsters' attention while you cut. But such a job can pay very well, and parents are grateful.

Nursing Homes

The enormous increase in nursing homes and assisted living centers has created many places where you can be employed. If you like service work, you may want to work in a hospital or senior citizens' home, giving cosmetic services to elderly or incapacitated people. Your responsibilities would include shampooing, cutting, manicuring, and pedicuring. Many patients are unable to groom themselves, and your skills would be very needed and appreciated. Patience, once again, is critical.

Cruise Lines

You may wish to look into the cruise lines for employment. There are beauty salons on every luxury liner, and several beauticians, manicurists, facialists, and barbers are needed for each ship. There are also openings for makeup artists and stylists. If being at sea interests you, be sure to list all the possible jobs that you could fill when you apply. Tips are better than average, and benefits are very good. Unless you are working on a cruise ship, you will have all the free time you want while you are in home port. A cruise ship will keep you busy most of the time, as passengers live on board very much as they do in a hotel. You would still have some designated free time in each port.

Cosmetic Companies

The cosmetics industry sells billions of dollars worth of makeup and treatment products annually. If your main interest is makeup, your field is wide open. Every major cosmetic company is a potential employer. Contact several and get an idea of what will be available at the time you graduate. You may desire to do demonstration work. In this capacity, you would work in the cosmetics company school, where you would demonstrate the product and show the future sales corps how to apply makeup or treatment products. There are various jobs open to the makeup artist. Demonstration is only the beginning, though you could make a career of doing just that. Your job can be as elaborate as your creative capabilities will permit. You could be a color adviser, and through your own familiarity with shading, shape, texture, and blending, work your way up the ladder. Experience is extremely critical, and your own artistic and creative abilities will dictate how well you will be paid. With the development of an artist's eye, you may become a makeup specialist.

Makeup artists often have fun while being paid very well. Though the top jobs, of course, are very limited, the makeup artists at the most expensive beauty salons and the people who make up the celebrities started out just as you are going to—at the bottom. Any extra art courses that you can take will be helpful. Many hours of practice will also make you more adept at applying makeup.

Fashionable boutiques hire makeup artists to acquaint their clientele with the latest products and their uses. Even pharmacies have job openings for makeup sales and demonstration. There are many overlapping positions in makeup and sales, and the employer should tell you if any certification or license is required.

Makeup artists could be called to work at a live modeling show, theater, department store, beauty salon, promotional show such as a hairdresser's convention or product promotion for television, or almost anywhere in the world where beauty is of interest. On-location work could take you to any country. Catalog work alone could keep you very busy. It takes many years to be in demand as a known makeup artist, but the work is available and your ambition and talents will be your guide.

Cosmetic companies usually place help-wanted ads, but if you have decided to go into facial work, contact one of the companies directly. You can call or write for an appointment. Tell them about your interests, qualifications, and experience, as well as your schooling and licenses or certifications. Have a well-written, attractive résumé to leave with the personnel interviewer. There are many assistantships in large companies, and working as an assistant could be a way for you to reach your final goal.

Barber Shops and Men's Hair Salons

The 54,000 barber–hairstylists in the United States have found work in barber shops, unisex shops, hotels, department stores, and specialty shops. There are many small businesses that cut men's hair. A visit to inquire about future employment may be your best course. There are barbers who work on men, women, and even children. Your work as a unisex stylist would permit you to practice anywhere that a cosmetology license is not required.

Positions in Beauty Salons

It takes many people to run a beauty salon with efficiency. Positions have become more and more specialized, and as a result the number of people who work in cosmetology has increased. The beauty salon hires as many operators and unlicensed persons as are needed to attract clients. Some salons need the talents of one type of technician only, such as a fast haircut shop, while others hire the full complement of every variety of hairstylist, colorist, nail specialist, facialist, barber/stylist, salesperson, and makeup artist.

The checkroom attendant takes your coat and gives you a dressing gown. The receptionist greets and books all the appointments. These are not cosmetologists but are positions critical to the business when you own your own salon. If the shop is very small, one person could fill all of these positions just to keep it running.

Beautician's Assistant

Beautician's assistants are usually apprentices who hold a state license. Requirements vary from state to state. An apprentice is frequently paid a small amount while polishing his or her skills as a stylist, hair colorist, or permanent-wave specialist. Beautician's assistants do shampoos, massage scalps, hold rollers, blow-dry hair, remove rollers, and brush hair off the patron for final cleanup. An assistant neither cuts hair nor does any actual hairstyling, but observes the hairstylist and receives on-the-job training. This is a good way to make a name for yourself in a better salon where the highest salaries and tips are earned. As an assistant you could expect to be paid around $150, plus tips, per week. Some salons will not pay that much, but the education you get as an assistant is similar to advanced education. The more that a hairstylist knows, the higher his or her salary.

Hair Coloring and Permanent Specialists

Good hair colorists are much in demand, as most women and many men at some time or other dye their hair. There are several types of hair color. Temporary colors are called tints and can be shampooed out. For the patron who is not ready for the dramatic leap to hair dyeing, a rinse or tint is the answer. A color rinse is great for making grey hair blend or to give highlights. It is not an overall solid color, as is dye. Hair dyeing and bleaching can take many years of training. A thorough understanding of chemicals is critical. Patch tests must be done on every patron to check for possible allergic reaction. The hair colorist does semipermanent and permanent hair colors, hennas, highlighting, retouching, lightening, toning, frosting, streaking, tipping, and hair painting. All of these different processes take many years to master. Assistants work alongside experienced hair colorists to learn the craft of hair coloring.

When dyeing hair, timing is of the utmost importance. Even though hair colorists use timers, they must concentrate their attention on the patrons. Serious damage could occur to the hair if the dye is left on too long. Hair colorists earn the highest salaries, anywhere from $600 to $3,000 per week and upward, plus tips, depending on their particular place of business.

Permanent waving, hair pressing, and chemical hair relaxing are all specialties. The size of the salon and the volume of business will dictate how many of these professionals are employed in a salon. Most specialists are able to command a salary of at least $600 to $750 a week. Again, it depends on whether or not he or she is paid a straight salary, a commission, or a combination of the two. Tips are usually excellent in any good hair salon, and the more specialized the service, the higher the tips.

Manicurists

Manicurists and pedicurists also have their places of employment in beauty salons. Patrons sometimes have these services done while their hair is being dried. Pedicurists normally work in a sectioned-off area to give the patron more privacy.

As a manicurist, your weekly salary could be any amount depending upon creative talents and your own ability to attract customers. You will have to advise your clients how to protect their nails by wrapping them, how to strengthen the vulnerable ends of long nails, and how a complete plastic nail can shield a badly broken nail until it has a chance to grow out. A manicurist who merely cleans, trims, and polishes nails will earn much less than one who is competent in creatively reconstructing nails or airbrushing them.

In New York City, a manicurist may earn as much as $700 a week, plus tips. A pedicurist, who, by the way, makes a higher per-client income, may earn from $20 per hour upward.

Makeup and Facial Specialists

Facial experts and makeup artists could be employed in a large salon or a day spa offering full services to the patrons. Services in these establishments would include leg waxing, facial massage, facial masques, wig styling, and even salespeople/cosmetologists demonstrating luxurious products to patrons. Many makeup artists freelance and do on-the-premises work like shows and weddings. Transportation and travel time has to be taken into consideration if you are to work on your own.

Hairstylists

The most prestigious and most recognized operators in any beauty salon are hairstylists. These men and women are highly skilled and well-trained experts in cutting hair in particular hairstyles. Haircutting is the most difficult part of handling hair. Hair can have different textures such as wiry, slippery, thick, fine, coarse, limp, and curly. Hair is a challenge to control, and haircuts train hair to lie in a desired manner. Top stylists can and do earn salaries commensurate with their abilities. Haircuts alone in New York City can cost up to $100. The average hairstylist there earns about $60 per cut, plus tips. Arrangements vary from employer to employer. If you are working for yourself, the sky is the limit for your potential income, as you do not give half to an employer.

Retail Sales

Most of the more famous salons promote their own cosmetic and hair products. Depending on how large the retail aspect of their business is, many salons actually have a salesperson in the employ of the salon. If there is no specific salesperson, the operator who recommends the special hair treatment or shampoo will receive commission on the sale. The beauty salon, of course, covers its cost and a small commission as well. Many specialists sell almost all of the creams, lotions, packs, scrubs, astringents, cleansers, and makeup that they use in the salon itself. Once the client is introduced to the product and is given instruction on how to apply it, he or she can do the same service at home. A shampoo specialist usually recommends the type of shampoo and rinse needed for a customer's particular scalp, and more often than not, these products are sold in the beauty shop. Product lines have been expanded to include the salon's own hairdryers, combs, styling brushes, and even bags large enough to carry all the products.

Manicuring specialties and different products used to make the nails stronger and keep them from looking unkempt are also sold in beauty salons. These creams are applied daily to supplement the once-a-week visit to the manicurist.

Wigs and postiches are often sold in beauty salons as well as all the required accessories, such as wig spray, carrier cases, brushes, and even clips and bows. These items can increase the income of the salon tremendously. If a salon services wigs and postiches, it would be a mistake not to sell them. The profit is very high on both natural and synthetic pieces.

Most women and men who have just come from a hairstylist's care and look their best will assume that part of the result is the product the hairstylist used. The psychology of selling the product right there is very powerful. If you suggest to your client that she or he go out and purchase the items that you have used in their treatment, chances are small that they will even remember the name of the product, let alone the procedure. Having the products accessible is only good business and good treatment for your client. Many salon patrons believe that it was not their weekly visit to the hairstylist that was too expensive for their budget but all those irresistible little goodies that added up to a very sizable income for the salon owner.

Managers and Manager-Operators

The managing cosmetologist (manager-operator) is often considered the intermediate post between doing cosmetological work and owning a salon. Each state dictates prerequisites, such as the amount of schooling needed, years of cosmetology experience, and manager-operator licensing. A manager-operator earns an annual income of about $28,000 in larger cities. The actual number of patrons whom a cosmetologist brings to the salon for weekly services has a great effect on his or her salary level.

Certain managerial positions are geared toward promotion, while others are strictly business coordination. The emphasis depends on the size of the salon and the salary arrangement.

The manager-operator must be licensed as a cosmetologist by the state in which he or she works. The manager-operator is permitted to touch the patron and do hairstyles, unlike the manager who is not a cosmetologist. States require varying levels of experience as a licensed operator before application can be made for the manager-operator license. Some states will permit operators to apply for that particular license as soon as they have started to work in a salon.

The advantage of having been an operator prior to taking a managerial position is that being familiar with all aspects of the cosmetology business is helpful in numerous ways. You may be permitted to suggest improvements, such as the introduction of new equipment or even a cosmetic line bearing your salon's signature. All of these factors directly influence your income.

A Manager's Responsibilities

As a manager you are directly responsible for the entire coordination and running of the business. Linens must be rented and laundered, supplies have to be kept in stock, and equipment has to be kept up-to-date and in state regulated working order. Your obligations would include seeing to all health and sanitation, licensing, and state regulations and keeping abreast of new codes. The decor of the salon may be one of your responsibilities. You must learn to balance economy with attractive surroundings.

Avoid being in a position where more and more work is expected of you without salary adjustments. You will be managing the largest portion of the business end of the salon. With the exception of rent or mortgage payments and directing funds for business expenses, you could conceivably be running the entire salon. You may even be managing the money for the owners. Coordinating the entire operation and suffering the headaches that accompany that amount of responsibility makes the manager's position the highest paid of the salon employees.

The wage scale varies from state to state and from salon to salon. Anything above minimum wage, and often well above $500 a week, can be expected in larger cities. The location of the salon will definitely have an influence on your salary. When customers are paying above average for services, the salary for a manager would be comparable. In a small local salon, the responsibilities may be of greater variety, but the pay would obviously have to be in line with the income of the shop.

Managers are normally expected to work the longest hours as well. A manager has to oversee the entire workings of the salon and must be aware of problems before they become too difficult to handle.

The hiring of personnel is very important. Keeping a happy, congenial group must always be paramount in the manager's mind. One unpleasant employee, no matter how talented, can cause miserable working conditions for everyone in the salon.

The quality of the workmanship is what will make or break your salon's future. If you have skilled hairstylists, word of mouth will interest others and your clientele will increase.

Another of the manager's responsibilities is to make certain that all licenses are current for every operator, the salon, and, of course, for himself or herself if the state requires a manager's license. Diplomat, overseer, personnel coordinator, inventory controller, host, record and schedule keeper—these all fall within the domain of the manager.

The positions open to managers are few. Many salon owners prefer to manage their own salons. If you are interested in management, consult trade periodicals and the want ads in large-city newspapers.

Beauty Salon Ownership

Beauty salon ownership may or may not be a goal in your cosmetological career. Many salon owners are not cosmetologists; they are businesspeople only. The expenses today of running a salon could well be a delineating factor, and for some operators the freedom from having to always keep abreast of the economy is a big consideration. If you own your own beauty salon, you have the opportunity to make greater financial gains, but if things do not go well, you will have to address all the losses. Even the most successful beauty salons have at times been forced to reduce their fees to clients due to slumps in the economy. The fluctuation of client fees for services tells you how well the beauty salon is doing in today's market. All of us need the services of hairdressers, and when you notice a price reduction in a haircut or a colorist's fees, you are made aware of an astute business move being made and know that good managerial talents are looking after the survival of the salon.

Current statistics show that one-third of the working licensed cosmetologists (about 263,300 operators nationwide) own and work in their own salons. The majority of these are hairstylists. These statistics still indicate that advancement in the field of cosmetology involves owning your own salon. The obvious attraction is that you will be your own boss and you will reap more of the profits. Drawbacks are financial responsibilities if the business does not succeed.

Salon owners can earn a salary of between $25,000 and $250,000 annually, depending upon the salon's location and the number of steady clients.

When you are enrolled in cosmetology school, you will likely have several hours of instruction in owning and managing a beauty salon. In New York State, about 50 hours are devoted to this area in the private beauty-school curriculum. Astute planning is of the utmost importance, as many complications can develop in trying to coordinate a project of this size. The tiniest salon with an area to service two patrons at a time will have all the major problems of a larger one. The difference will be the dispersal of responsibility among the larger staff in a bigger salon.

You will be responsible for everything, even if you do have a manager and a very competent staff. Ultimately, as the owner, you are responsible to the state and to all of your salon's patrons, whether you actually work on the person or one of your employees does. You will be responsible for insurance coverage, rental payments, salaries, hiring, firing, accounting, paying taxes on the business, and purchasing all the supplies. If you do not want to handle the day-to-day operations of your salon, you can delegate these jobs to a manager-operator who is qualified to manage a salon. This person should have many years of experience as a licensed cosmetologist and must be qualified for a managerial position. It is very difficult to run an entire operation without responsible help. A good manager with a charismatic personality can make or break your beauty salon. A pleasant, attractive, well-groomed, intelligent, warm, and efficient person can coordinate the entire business, making it an enjoyable environment for workers and patrons alike.

Beauty School Ownership

Beauty schools can be privately owned or part of a franchise operation where many schools are in the possession of a large business. These schools can be very successful; with all the new laws there are nail schools, aestheticians' schools, and electrologists' schools teaching their fields exclusively.

Graduates in these areas number in the tens of thousands annually. With tuition costs ranging from $2,000 for a license in manicuring to $10,000 for one in hairstyling, you can see that these are solid businesses.

The establishment and operation of cosmetology schools is regulated by state codes that address virtually every aspect of owning these businesses. You will need to understand and adhere to all of these regulations to run a legal, successful school.

4

ADDITIONAL BEAUTY INDUSTRY JOBS

BEAUTY EXTENDS BEYOND the parameters of the hairstylist or hair colorist, or even the manicurist/pedicurist. This chapter describes some other areas in the field of cosmetology that you may be interested in pursuing.

Aestheticians and Facialists

Pampered female travelers now demand that American salons keep up with their international counterparts. Facials used to be the least utilized of the beauty services as they were thought to be purely cosmetic; however, they are now recognized for their therapeutic value. Asians and Europeans treasured the effects of a facial on their skin and raised the facial to a near-scientific level. Americans, known for their fascination with hair and makeup, had no interest in the facial salon until recently. Now it is commonplace in such salons to offer a complete range of services—from herbal to electrical-appliance facials.

People with a public image to maintain know the wonderful benefits of facial deep-pore cleansing and a relaxing facial massage. Facials fall in the category of definite pampering as they feel luxurious, but the truth is that your facial skin needs more than soap and water to battle the foul air that we live in. Many a movie star credits her flawless skin to her facialist and considers those visits to be just as critical as any other cosmetological one. It is interesting to note that just a few years ago there were a handful of skin care salons that basically promoted their own skin products. Demand for total beauty care has forced the bigger salons to include aestheticians among their offerings. If a salon has a small but sophisticated following, it would not be uncommon to find the manicurist or makeup artist doing facial work, which could be a consideration as a career choice.

Younger people as well are taking advantage of facials. There are many teenagers who have problem skin and are helped greatly by thorough skin cleansing that can be done only by professionals with the knowledge and experience of dealing with their skin difficulties. Skin care has come into its own, with more than 13,000 facialists practicing today. This expansion has caused much specialization within the area.

The Need for Facial Specialists

Skin of leather consistency is caused by too much of any natural element. Unprotected skin will form a heavy and darker texture to save itself from further damage. Sadly, more often than not, damaged skin is permanent. Skin dried out from too much sun will never be soft or delicate again. We know that a little direct sunlight is vital, but it must be acquired gradually. If our faces were not constantly exposed, we would not need highly specialized techniques to protect this vulnerable area. Grime and dirt attack our faces and hands. But hands have tougher skin than faces, and gloves and mittens at least partially protect hands during many times of the year. Yet the most delicate of skin areas is expected to meet all kinds of weather and remain attractive, young, and as unlined as possible.

There are many ways to retain moisture in the skin, keep facial muscles toned and exercised, and remove dirt and excessive oil from the face. The specialist who is most knowledgeable in this field will not only have a cosmetologist's license but will have had several weeks of intensive schooling in highly skilled techniques.

Even if a person is not troubled with any particular skin problems and has the luck to have absolutely radiant skin, the services of a skin specialist can ward off potential trouble through skin analysis, helping the skin to stay as young as physically possible.

Skin care is also known as aesthetics. If someone specializes in the care of the skin, he or she could be known as a cosmetician, a skin care analyst, an aesthetician, a skin therapist, or a skin specialist. When you are looking for work, you could conceivably be listed as any of these and still work exclusively with the face.

After you complete your state boards you will be a licensed cosmetologist. In some states you will go directly into facial specialty work without further instruction. Some states require that you obtain a specialty certificate. In New York, for example, you need both the certificate and the state license to land a good job with higher pay and more opportunity for advancement. But you can get a job doing facials in a beauty salon with just your state licensing. In general, if you want to specialize, try to get as much instruction as you can afford from as highly recognized an authority as possible. Education is the fastest and surest way up the professional ladder. One word of recommendation from a well-known figure in your chosen field can be extremely valuable.

Education for Facial Specialists

Basic skin care is covered in beauty school training where you learn how to manually cleanse, manipulate, and massage the skin. You will have a little skin analysis, some anatomy and physiology pertaining to the skin, and a brief course on diseases of the skin. It is critical that you understand all the possible disorders of the skin for health precautions. You should also know your limitations in being able to determine whether a minor case of acne can be corrected or whether a doctor's advice is needed. You must be able to identify a bump or lump on or beneath the skin's surface before you apply anything to the client's skin. It could be a harmless fatty cyst or something infectious that could be contagious to you or other patrons.

Familiarize yourself with the skin's functions and conditions so that you can advise your clients on preventive or corrective measures. Many clients have similar problems. Younger people have skin that tends to be too oily, while middle-aged skin is too dry. It is pleasurable to have the skin manipulated at any age, and a variety of massages are indicated by skin types. Some forms of massage are relaxing and some are stimulating. The muscles of the face benefit from the effects of a massage. Tensions and stress show on the face more than on any other part of the body. Massage can reduce stressful feelings by causing tension to disappear. Tight muscles can also be therapeutically relaxed with heat and light. Some techniques employ several processes in one treatment. You might have electric massage (stimulation) with heat, or, after an application of an abrasive cream, steam might be prescribed. Chemical reactions speed up with the addition of heat. If the opposite treatment is called for, astringents cool and close pores. A skilled skin specialist can teach you how to take the best care of your skin. Cleaning your type of skin can be more complex than just using soap and water, and you could be harming your skin by not giving it the proper care it needs.

Most states require 300 to 900 hours for licensure. Some states also require a high school education before you can enroll in a skin care school. The approximate cost for tuition in such a school runs from $2,500 to $7,500 for 600 hours, depending upon the state. This would be a complete program for makeup techniques and facial procedures. There are private schools where your costs are the highest, but these courses are also offered in some public high schools where you could be looking at virtually no cash outlay.

Close to half of the states have made a distinction between a cosmetology license and a facial care or aesthetician's license. Upon completion of an average of 600 hours of schooling in facial care, you could be a fully qualified specialist in these states. You would still have to pass your exams, but not the extended ones set up by the cosmetology boards. Your work would be restricted to facial care and makeup.

Makeup Artists

This rapidly expanding area of cosmetology is seeing a 10 percent annual growth. If you have an artistic flair and a desire to create special effects, you may be very well rewarded as a makeup artist. Most people know if they like what they see, but they do not know what made this occur. Individual lessons or a professional application of makeup for an occasion can be very expensive. But more and more clients are demanding perfection, and that means lots more positions will be available for makeup artists.

One specialty of the recognized makeup artist is wedding parties. In the New York area, it would not be unusual to pay several hundred dollars for the talents of a known artist for just one face.

Makeup artists are highly recognized today as respected professionals in the beauty industry. The demand for them is shared between actors and actresses and the public need to correctly apply the thousands of cosmetic products that confront the baffled purchaser. With plastic surgery, a whole new aspect of makeup has emerged, and the makeup artist has dozens of clever tricks and illusions to communicate to the client.

A makeup specialist's first responsibility to his or her patrons is to analyze their skin and advise them how to clean it correctly. Everyone has a different skin type, and the balance between the skin's natural oils and what is applied externally is important. If you have skin that lacks moisture and oils, you will follow a program designed to save the resources that are already in scarce supply. If your skin is very oily, it is unlikely that all areas of your face are in that condition. A specialist's analysis is a form of advice to the patron. When a specialist sees flakes of dry skin around a client's nose, for example, he or she would recommend removing those dead skin cells so that the underlying cells can breathe. Contrary to belief, dry skin that is flaking does not indicate lack of oils, but the opposite. Stimulation to that area is needed so that dead cells are naturally sloughed off.

Skin Care

Communication is vital. It is important for makeup specialists to clearly explain what problems they recognize in a customer's skin and how a beauty program is to be followed for best results. Your professional eye will have to quickly analyze any problems and advise the patron of the most efficient way to deal with them. Your ability to save patrons time in their daily cleansing routine is very important. If they have to allot more time than is practical in their daily routine, they may not complete it. If so, the skin will suffer. If an individual takes preventions when young, healthy and supple skin can exist well past middle age.

Color

There are two ways in which color can work to improve the facial appearance. The first is by altering the contour of the bones of the face. Every face is unequal in its two halves. Your job would be to see what is uneven and shade or add color as the fault dictates.

Color can be used to correct facial defects by concealing certain "bad colors." If dark circles, sallowness, or ruddiness dominate a face, careful selection of concealers and foundations can alter them. Concealers also can cover small scars or blemishes. Heavy makeup is not only extremely unattractive but also very bad for the skin's ability to breathe. A touch of color is enough to achieve the effect of natural good looks. Remember that you are teaching someone how to improve his or her skin's color, so explanations are necessary. Really make an effort to explain what you are doing in terms your patron will understand and remember how to emulate.

Wide varieties of cosmetic products are used to blend and highlight different facial features. The eyes are the most expressive facial feature, and because they are often smaller than we would like them to be, much concentration is put into eye makeup. Eye color can be enhanced and made more vibrant by adding eyeliner or eye shadow. The iris (the colored part of the eye) is affected by any color that it reflects. By clever use of shadows, eyes can be made to look closer together, farther apart, rounder, and larger. Great skill is needed to bring about these corrections, but with a light touch, you will be able to develop that talent in due time.

The overall look is the final goal. Nothing should stand out. The eyes, eyebrows, eyelids, cheeks, and lips should be highlighted, and the rest of the face should be a perfect, unflawed background to set off the features.

Education

There are several places where you can receive instruction to do makeup. Many cosmetic companies train and develop talents through continued guidance and instruction, especially as their new products come out. Practice is the key word, and you will be expected to blend old products with new ones in actual makeup work.

Schooling could be as little as a week in length, and you are expected to gain your experience on the job. You obviously cannot learn makeup in a week, so observing the more experienced makeup person's technique is invaluable. You usually are asked to do very minimal work in actual application of makeup until you really start to have a feel for it.

You could opt to take your training in a school of aesthetics. There the course would be whatever the state required. One New York school has a program of 600 hours, and the tuition is currently $7,000. A license is required for graduates to work in New York State. In states that require licenses, schooling in cosmetics may be taken as a special course, or the whole cosmetology school training may be required.

Licensing

Cosmetology boards for makeup are a requirement in many states. In most states, a small number of school hours are set aside for the strict pursuit of skin analysis, corrective or complete makeup, or application of false eyelashes. You will notice that all of these require actually touching the patron, the point on which laws differ. In some states, you cannot touch the patron without a license, and in other states, as long as the service is performed only on the skin's surface (such as with makeup or electrology), a license is not required. There is no consistency in the states' prohibitions. Certain services that are considered purely cosmetic in some states are regulated by medical boards in others.

Jobs in Makeup

After your education as a makeup person, you could seek employment almost anywhere in department stores, drugstores, cosmetic company demonstrations on various locations, beauty salons, specialty shops, promotionals, beauty shows, modeling shows, theaters, television, and movies sets. Some jobs available are in the sales area of cosmetic companies. This is often the springboard for many career jobs in cosmetics.

Pay scales vary greatly depending on which position you take. But starting pay is almost never below $400 a week. In large cities, pay would likely be more than $500. Your decision to work on commission and salary or just salary will affect your income, too.

Makeup is a rapidly expanding field, and hundreds of jobs occur with each new cosmetic company. You have a wide-open field from which to choose. You may select full- or part-time work, sales, demonstration, or even international sales. There is an opening in the cosmetic job market that could very likely satisfy you. New products are distributed in the most remote corners of the earth. As these products are distributed, they create jobs.

Electrologists

Permanent removal of hair by electrical processes is a much-used service due to its ultimate timesaving and end result. Many areas of the body are covered with unwanted hair—upper lip, arms, legs, personal areas, and even the hairline. When the hours and expense of using gels, depilatories, disposable razors, and waxing services are added up, it often makes more sense to seek a once-and-for-all solution. Though a little uncomfortable for the client, electrolysis is good for a lifetime, and in this age of timesaving, it is the paramount technique of choice. There are many places where you could find the services of an electrologist—in day spas, beauty salons, or in specialty boutiques of their own.

The removal of unwanted hair by electrolysis involves permanently removing the hair follicle with an electrical current. Make an appointment with a professional operator if you think that you may be interested in a career in this area of cosmetology. Salespeople who sell the electrical equipment used in this process quite frequently run the schools that teach electrolysis. Some beauty schools do teach electrology, but since there is no licensing required in many states, not all schools offer the course in their curriculum.

Electrologists learn how to insert a very fine needle or wire into a hair follicle. The needle (contrary to popular belief) never punctures the skin. It is merely inserted in the natural opening of the hair follicle. A gentle electrical current is then applied to the papilla (hair cell). As a result of this process, the papilla dies and the hair is then removed with tweezers. An electrologist works with a large magnifying glass that has a light around its circumference. There is a certain amount of eyestrain in this job because electrologists must concentrate on one hair at a time. After you build up your finger dexterity, you will be able to remove many hairs in a few minutes. The needle is held in one hand while you spread or stretch the skin gently with the other hand. While looking through the magnifying glass, you will be able to quickly guide the needle into the hair follicle.

Education

Electrolysis is still considered the safest method of permanent hair removal if performed by a qualified electrologist with up-to-date electric equipment. Therefore it is critical that you attend a good school of electrolysis. In the state of New York, you will need to attend classes to receive your certificate. The typical school requires 120 hours of work. The curriculum consists of lectures, actual clinic work with electrolysis machines and patrons, and testing. The current price of tuition at a school of electrology is around $3,500 for 300 hours. There are evening courses and even online courses, so you could conceivably have your certificate after three weeks of concentrated schooling.

Licensing

Electrology classes differ greatly from state to state. In Massachusetts, for example, 1,100 hours are required prior to taking a state board exam to practice electrolysis. In California, an electrology course of 600 hours taught by an established school of cosmetology or electrology must be completed before you can apply for state registration and licensure. Also, the age limit is 17, and a twelfth-grade education is a prerequisite for taking the course. So you can see state laws are drastically different in the field of electrolysis.

Finding a Job

Upon your graduation from electrology school, you will be able to find work in certain specialty shops, day spas, or your own private salon, if you want to set one up. Unlike the other career possibilities discussed in this chapter (with the possible exception of facial and skin care work), electrologists most often work for themselves. The equipment is minimal. All you need is a short-wave machine, a couch or hydraulic chair for your patron, something comfortable for you to sit on, magnifying lamps, needles and a needle sterilizer, tweezers, and a few antiseptic lotions. At a cost of $1,200 for the machine, you could be in business for yourself. This is obviously a perfect job for someone who wants to be his or her own boss. Your time is your own, and the average hourly charge for electrolysis can be anywhere from $60 to $200, depending on your area of the country.

Insurance costs for an independent electrologist in New York State are about $125 to $150 annually. This fee is so reasonable because there seem to be few malpractice suits. Even with the competition of laser hair removal, the field of electrology is wide open for earning. Large numbers of electrologists are not available, and the procedure of removing hair electrically is very time-consuming. There are therefore plenty of job opportunities in this necessary and rewarding field. Not everyone has heard of electrology, and with a little advertising and word-of-mouth praise from your patrons, you might easily establish a career for yourself in a very short time.

Competition Hairstylists

Hairstyle competition stylists learn how to prepare a model's hair with strict specifications for a particular look. Details are spelled out and experienced cosmetologists in the field then judge the contest. Competitions could be as simple as a daytime hairstyle for the office all the way to an exotic cut, color, and evening style with hair ornaments. It is educational and fun to attend these competitions just to observe the top technicians in your chosen field. Not only can you become inspired by their creativity, but you also can learn many tricks of the trade by watching their timesaving moves.

The reasons you might want to enter hairdressers' competitions would be if you were planning on making a career in hairstyling. You really should consider applying to as many competitions as possible. There are numerous benefits. You will meet respected people in your chosen field, and you will be able to observe firsthand the best cosmetologists. Exposure to many clever hairdressers is a tremendous learning experience.

You have the advantage of being able to enter competitions as early as during your days in beauty school. The confidence that you can gain in competition is worth every penny of your entrance fees. Competition prizes range from trophies to cash, and many contacts are made during these shows that can lead to recognition in the cosmetology world. The press covers all the proceedings, and many fine hairstylists have gained a following through competition.

Competitions

A cosmetology student would most likely compete in a daytime haircut, style, or other already familiar technique. The experience of competing gives the student a better idea of accuracy, speed, and the correct method of attaining an end result at someone's request. When the pressure is on, some students function at their best. Others simply cannot cope with all the confusion and noise and are better off in the slower pace of school. This does not mean that if you have trouble at your first competition you should not consider entering competitions in the future, after you have gained experience and confidence.

There are also competitions for students of barbering schools who must quickly and skillfully perform a man's cut and present their model with a final polished look. The haircut itself may be judged separately.

Competitions are sponsored by a variety of groups. The most common sponsor is the larger manufacturer of products like hairdressings or makeup, publishers of cosmetology magazines, and affiliations of cosmetologists. Competitions occur frequently. To find these, look in local papers and log onto your local cosmetology website.

Areas of Competition

One specialty for competition is permanent waving. There are many ways in which hair can be set and styled to achieve a particular look. The choice of wrapping method makes a remarkable difference. You could perm only the base of the hair, or only the ends of the hair, or the entire length of the hair. All of these techniques give a wide variety of hairstyles and enable you to achieve innovative results.

Time allotment is critical, so have everything organized in your mind ahead of time. Judges are usually a panel of several authorities in the field. You will be told the theme or silhouette to be achieved and whether it is to be a daytime or evening hairstyle. Be certain that you and your model are available at the prescribed hour, as latecomers are turned away and your entrance fee probably will not be refunded.

Some possible competitions could be creative coloring, creative or "open" hairstyling (the contestant can create any style or type of hair design such as high fashion, day, or evening), men's styling competition by a cosmetologist (no barbers permitted to enter), creative cutting, or dual competition, wherein one male and one female model are styled by the same contestant to show the operator's ability to "cross over." (Formerly, "unisex" was the term used to describe hairstyling for both men and women.) There are competitions wherein the contestant coordinates hair, makeup, and even clothing to present a total look.

The Platform Hairstylist

Hair product manufacturers hire platform hairstylists to demonstrate their wares to beauty schools, beauty salons, and the public via hair shows. These very talented artists work with hair and all its associated accoutrements such as dyes, cuts, styles, and the newest trends. As specialists they command very high salaries and are often paid per-hour wages of $100 to $300. The creative ability of the platform artist sets him or her apart from other cosmetologists by the highly polished technical work that is accomplished quickly and with near-perfect results. This stylist thus becomes a liaison between the world of newly created fashion and the world of the cosmetologists who must re-create this look for the public, their clients.

The Role of the Platform Stylist

It is financially impossible for all the cosmetologists to return to school as often as hair fashions change. With a platform stylist visiting and teaching in the beauty salon, everyone benefits. Operators do not have to lose even a day's work, since the platform stylist is usually scheduled to give lectures and demonstrations directly after the salon's business hours. By being in the work environment, the operator can more easily visualize how and with what equipment new hairstyles will be created. Busier salons can afford to have a few operators ask the platform stylist questions during lengthier sessions as other operators continue to work. Some instructors do platform stylist work as well as beauty school instruction on an advanced level. There are many ways in the beauty industry to combine the various aspects of the cosmetology trade, as long as you are practicing in a state that does not require more education than you have or a different license from the one that you hold.

Working as a Platform Stylist

Platform stylists can expect to earn between $500 and $1,000 for a day's instruction. Supply houses, cosmetic firms, and sometimes affiliates sponsor platform stylists. A normal schedule for a well-qualified platform stylist might be giving lectures and instruction only twice a month. It is not an everyday job, and some of these "teachers" work in managerial or operator positions in salons. Platform stylists take their lecture, instruction, slides, and models from place to place. But their schedule is almost never full-time.

Another advantage of working as a platform stylist is the potential for travel. Extensive travel may not be necessary. If you want to stay in a limited vicinity, taking your newly learned knowledge to an area with a smaller radius, you could conceivably stay within several counties or states. Perhaps you could find yourself lecturing in other countries. As fashion travels, so must hairstyle techniques. We in the United States often adapt French or English hair fashions. This offers a great opportunity for the platform stylist to learn the method and transport it.

Finding a Job

On occasion a platform stylist can find work through first establishing himself or herself as a competition stylist. The demand for his or her work could eventually lead to actual platform work when available. Work as a platform stylist also can be acquired through hiring a booking agent. Some stylists simply freelance if their contacts are already established through a hairdressing affiliate.

In certain states a platform license is required. This license is applied for only once and lasts for as long as the stylist maintains an active cosmetology license.

Wigs, Hairpieces, and Hair Enhancement

Due to chemotherapy and its side effect of baldness, we have seen a tremendous demand for hair replacement. Men as well as women are looking toward buying hair in the form of wigs, add-ons, wiglets, postiches, toupees, switches, falls, and hair extensions. Hair can be surgically replaced as well, but often this method is obvious by the sparse growth and visible scalp, punctuated at quarter-inch intervals. The preferred methods most often are the less expensive cosmetological ones.

Hair extension is extraordinarily popular, and given the current rates, a specialty in this area would guarantee an income in the range of $150,000 to $200,000 a year. It would have the potential of becoming intriguing work due to the many visible clients you could be servicing. Exclusivity in hair extension procedures would mean that you would do the monthly maintenance on the add-on.

This is another area of solid income as the upkeep for each client would be around $50 to $100 per visit. Hair extensions grow along with your own hair, to which they are attached, and thus need more specialized care than your own natural hair.

Choosing a Wig

Wigs have become a major necessity for chemotherapy patients and this has opened a huge market. The two kinds of hair available for wigs are natural and synthetic. A natural wig made of real human hair is the first choice. Human hair used in wigs and hairpieces is chemically boiled to remove the color and dyed to match a color wheel that gives a precise choice to the patron. In the case of medical need, a patient often cuts his or her own hair before it starts to fall out, and a wig is fashioned from it. This type of wig runs between $6,000 and $10,000, as it is custom made.

Wigs must be carefully fitted to the patron's head. If it is too large, applying hot or warm water to the cap and leaving it to dry on a block smaller than the patron's head can actually shrink it. Tucks also can be taken in the cap of the wig to make it the correct size. A new kind of wig has strips of hair held together by elastic. This wig is lighter and lets air reach the scalp because the hair is not a solid mass, like it is in the traditional style.

The wig made of synthetic hair has its limitations; synthetic hair often is used in less expensive wigs. Modacrylic fibers are supposedly so cleverly used now that synthetic wigs can look very natural. Of course, the actual construction of the wig itself can dictate the quality of the wig. Hand-tied wigs are the best quality, while machine-made ones are less desirable.

The cost of cleaning the two types relates to the original cost of the wig. The less expensive synthetic wig can be washed in ordinary shampoo and rinsed in water. The natural hair wig is cleaned with a fluid similar to dry cleaning fluid. This fluid is dangerous and must be used in a ventilated area.

Care of natural hair wigs is so extensive that the cost is much higher than that for a synthetic wig. The natural hair must be conditioned, as natural oils must be cleaned out of the wig along with dirt. Gentle care will guarantee a long life to a real hair wig. It can even be dyed; the synthetic wig cannot.

Hairpieces come in varying sizes and lengths. Women use them for special effects, to give more height or weight to their own hair, or to fill in sparse areas. Hairpieces can be made of artificial or natural hair by machine or by hand.

Working as a Wig Stylist

Wig stylists fit, clean, cut, style, and comb out wigs and hairpieces. Packaging the wig in a carrier may also be a duty, as most patrons never come to the wig stylist, and the stylist must pack and send the wig back to the customer.

A wig stylist who works in a beauty salon may need a license as a cosmetologist. Often a wig specialist certificate is adequate to work on wigs in salons, department stores, specialty shops, or costume departments. State health codes set strict standards for wig handlers. No wig is permitted to touch another wig, and all wigs must be handled so that they are not contaminated by anything that touches them. The block that the wig rests on, the pins that hold it, and the rollers, clips, brushes, or combs that may come in contact with it must all be carefully sanitized.

Wig styling is covered in New York State licensing for cosmetologists. This permits the wig stylist to actually work on the wig or hairpiece while it is on the patron. Not all wig stylists need to touch the patron, and each stylist has to decide whether he or she needs that extra licensing. If a person is merely selling wigs, it is highly unlikely that any certification would be required in any state, though he or she may wish to combine actual hairpiece work and wig styling. The particular question of who must be licensed for wig work is undecided. The answer seems to depend on whom a stylist is working for, where he or she is working, and if he or she has to touch the client.

Selling Hairpieces to Men

For many reasons, men use hairpieces as much or more than women. Advertisements are everywhere for hairpieces for men who are balding or have had chemotherapy. Toupees are mentioned briefly here, as they are similar to, but not quite the equivalent of, the postiche for a woman, and you may or may not need licensing in your particular state to handle toupees. It all depends on the laws that cover your state's barbering codes and if hairpieces are regulated under your state's law. In New York City, licensing is needed, as measurements for wigs require touching the patron, which is the deciding factor. Cosmetology boards do not regulate men's hairpieces. So though it is highly unlikely that if you work as a cosmetologist you would be doing men's hairpieces, you might be employed in a unisex salon where the question may arise. It is your job to be able to advise your patron, and you should be able to recommend a reliable men's hair care professional.

5

AN OVERVIEW OF THE
MODELING INDUSTRY

TODAY MORE THAN ever, modeling has become coveted as a get-rich-quick profession. Particularly among very young women, the idea of celebrity modeling has taken on a whole new reverence. International arenas are encompassing artists' models, runway models, photographic models, promotional models, television and video models, and showroom models. For a job that is surely short-lived (most models are has-beens by age 30) it is amazing to see the hordes of those desiring to become models. The gamut covers every age and every ethnic group, as anyone is a potential model. Artists and photographers enlist a wide range of models in all sizes and shapes. If you are truly determined to be a professional model, you probably will find some work in one capacity or another. Commercial artists work with the tiniest babies to the most aged grandparents, with the thinnest to the most corpulent bodies, and with the entire spectrum of ethnic backgrounds.

Artists' Models

Posing for an artist entails being a figure or a face that inspires that artist's creativity. What appeals to the artist's taste or is needed to depict a certain idea will dictate what is required in the live model. Every body type and age group is included as the artist seeks inspiration.

Artists' models often start working in local art schools or for private painters, sculptors, or photographers as children. Working for an artist gives valuable training in discipline while teaching the model a bit about color, line, and style, if they are at all observant. The work entails holding a given pose for approximately five minutes, and then, after a short break, the pose is resumed. This can be very tedious to most individuals, and it is a very good test of potential patience for a future in modeling. If you are bored beyond belief, you'll not only have a tough time as a model regardless of the earnings, but you will not be a good model to the artist.

You must be available until the artistic rendering is completed, and that could be as short as a few hours or as long as a several months. Your patience and professionalism are critical, as many artists have that infamous artistic temperament. If you want the job, you'll have to be the one to comply, as most artists have very powerful personalities and strong convictions as to how their art will progress.

Available work can be found where artists gather, such as art schools, private galleries and studios, and classes held in art museums. Contact these directly and follow their directions as far as getting an interview or an actual tryout in front of a group of art students. Often there is work to be found at college and university art and photographic classes. One job always leads to the next, so if you are mainly interested in remuneration from the modeling work, a little ingenuity is necessary. Fashion institutes hire many models, and here is where the need becomes more specific. A female model must have the current fashion figure as well as poise and perhaps a bit of individual character. Often she must supply her own fashion wardrobe used in the model-sketching classes. Illustration classes also demand that the model use her own wardrobe.

The pay scale in the New York area is around $15 an hour at the entry level for the art schools and around $25 an hour for illustration classes. Different types of schools and individual artists pay varied scales as well. You will have to decide what you need and can afford to live on.

Illustrators' Models

Illustrators are a special kind of artist used in the fashion field to depict a more aesthetic face and figure than nature intended. He or she can and does make a drawing of someone taller than a tree and skinnier than a strand of angel hair pasta. It is amazing to see the human model who sat for the rendering become totally stylized in the finished product.

As a fashion illustrator's model, you will be paid very well. Some illustrators pay in the hundreds, while famous ones pay models thousands of dollars for a layout. If a celebrity model is used, her enormous pay scale would be met here as well. Some illustrators work from a photograph of the model, while others like to use the live model to view the different angles and present several renditions to the client. It is often believed to be quite prestigious to work with the world's top fashion illustrators as they are recognized artists and their work is very respected.

Promotional Models

Hundreds of these live models sell everything from cosmetics to cars. This is one of the fastest-growing areas in the modeling world. Huge makeup companies were the first to see the potential for larger sales by having the model wear the products and also personally hawk the items. Specialty shops and department stores in New York City alone engage hundreds of these promo models every day. Most of them are not subtle in their approach. With atomizer in hand and free gift-with-purchase enticements, you are inundated with hordes of these models. So much selling has come to be done in this manner that the ranks now entail live models as well as promotional personnel. The model is selected to be more or less the image that the company is trying to establish with the use of its product.

Men, too, are employed by clothing/perfume makers for men. They wear some costume to link them to the product's theme and try to catch your attention with their attire and giveaways. The employment level here is still very much on the rise. Even the most humble of the clothing manufacturers now are promoting perfumes, where the really big money is to be made.

Established promotional shows like the ones held at the Jacob Javits Center in New York City also hire live models. These shows are seasonal and pay better than most other promotional modeling due to the short but intense period of work. Some verbal skill is required here. You may do as little as answer questions about a yacht that you are babysitting, or you may need to know every minute detail about a canned speech. Whatever the client needs, you'll have to be flexible enough to provide. It is not unusual to be on some sort of commission as well as salary if you are a promotional model. In general, this type of model is hired when new products need to be presented to the public—by week or month. A ballpark figure is around twenty dollars to several hundred dollars an hour for a very chic product promoted by a recognized model. Benefits could ensue if you became the prime spokesperson/model for a specific product.

To land a promotional modeling job, peruse the Internet, contact companies and department stores, and read the trade papers. They will guide you in the right direction.

Garment or Fit Models

Seventh Avenue between the high 20s and the low 40s in New York City is known as the garment district. Within this section nearly all the high-priced clothing made in the United States will be produced. The names that you recognize as "designer" manufacturers will be found here. It is very common for a patternmaker to select one girl for that house's size for its sample.

Fit models are usually about five feet nine inches tall and weigh about 118 pounds, ideally. This allows for a large variety in length of the torso and dimension of rib cage, bust, and hip. If you are seeking work as a fit model, look in the employment section of local newspapers.

Unglamorous work at best, you may find the employers are brusque or shockingly demanding. If you are well mannered, it might be a rude shock to work here, but the experience will help you assess your depth of desire to seek a modeling career. It is steady, pays the rent, and the good part is that if you can stand the pressure here, you can stand it anywhere. Jobs are generally by the week and pay approximately $100 to $150 per hour.

Seventh Avenue modeling is most beneficial if you can get work where you respect the designer and want to learn the ropes.

Some girls are clever enough to make the leap from showroom to runway at the time of the seasonal presentations. It's rare but not impossible.

Photographers' Models

The most desired job in the industry is photography work. The women who have reached the pinnacle of modeling are all in this category. These are also the preteens who are astounding themselves with their quarter-million-dollar-a-year salaries. They arrive in the largest cities in droves with fame and fortune on their minds. The competition has never been more fierce, nor the ladder more slippery. Modeling has become a road to riches for the eager and independent young neophyte.

Photographic models include everyone from the baby in diapers to the high fashion mannequin in the international marketplace. Catalog work is still among the most common bread-and-butter work for all ages, sexes, and ethnic groups. There is a new boom in the online mail-order catalog business, and it guarantees many jobs for models. The pay starts at around $150 per hour and goes up, depending on your fees commanded by the agency.

"Real" people are used in many catalogs now as opposed to a few years back, when, for example, a totally unbelievable scene showed a buxom blonde hand-mowing the lawn.

There are also "part" models. They may have perfect teeth for a toothpaste commercial, elegant long legs for a stocking ad, or luxuriant hair for a shampoo clip. The current rate for a hand model who is a member of the Screen Actors Guild is $445.30 per day. You can see how many niches there are in the photographic area of modeling. All of them pay exceedingly well, and many give you an introduction to the next job. Photographic work is available in the smallest town to the most sophisticated cities. The number of modeling agencies in Texas and Canada tripled in the last ten years, so the "part model" has a very good future.

Runway Models and Fashion-Show Work

Runway modeling continues to be a social event of the highest order. The queens of the runway shows include about a dozen high fashion divas who work every big-name designer's presentation in Paris and Italy. It is no wonder that supermodels command such high salaries, when the shows that they work draw masses of millionaires just dying to buy these garments before someone else does. When gowns sell for $350,000 each, you can understand the model who says that she is what made the gown look so desirable and, thus, demands her share, too.

Today's public wants to be the rich and the famous, and fashion makes them feel that this is attainable by copying runway clothes. The really great costumes that ensure the designer's creative recognition are rarely worn by anyone except the models, and the street gear is simply not as fantastic, stunning, or, frankly, as much fun to wear. It is not by accident that the couture designer presents the pièce de résistance in the form of a breathtaking, celestial wedding gown as the last statement in his or her collection. It is what fashion and modeling is all about—illusion at its most stellar level.

The fashion model who is invited to do the runway is certainly already a supermodel or nearing that status. These shows are patronized by not only those who can afford to buy the creations (though they are the most necessary) but by the fashion industry, its editors, its manufacturers, and its thousands of links in the chain: hair stylists, accessory makers, makeup artists, and armies of others who are attached to this area of chic.

Runway models are rarely teenagers; they are usually women in their early 20s who have had some serious experience. The casual strut dominating the runway comes from years of working what is familiarly referred to as the "catwalk." The near-bored-to-death glances from the models probably are more real than theatrical, but it's all part of the portrayal of the semijaded attitude so popular in status culture.

Different parts of the world offer different levels of runway work. You will be able to find these jobs in your local mall, in small cities at business lunches, for charities on hotel stages, in Seventh Avenue houses, and worldwide wherever fashion exists.

Runway models are the greatest beauties that the industry can find. These women are ultra-tall, leggy, lean, pretty, and have a full bosom. The male runway model must be slender, have nicely developed chest muscles, and be that near-classic size 40. He must exude a sexy quality, whatever that is defined as at the moment. Currently it is the unshaven movie-star look. Statistics show that American men purchase what they need and that fashion per se is only considered by one-fourth of them. With those numbers, is it any wonder that men's fashions are still primarily dress suits and jeans? There simply aren't as many opportunities for the male models as there are for the females.

Male Models

Although male models also ply the runways, rarely is there anywhere near the same hoopla for them as there is for women. They are, however, seen annually on the runways of Paris, Milan, and New York in innovative clothing at big designers' shows. There are simply no comparisons between the celebrity models who are all women and any of the male models. The public can name many of these lady divas, but the male model neither commands the runway nor the gigantic celebrity and its accompanying salaries. Image leads to income, and this is very much a female-beauty dominated world. According to one modeling association, the female model's income outranks the male's by 50 to 100 times per annum!

However, male models are making slow inroads into this female-dominated trade. There is more work now than ever for male models. With the advent of fashion shows and runway work, men are more visible, and they want the big salaries that women models have enjoyed for many years.

The female model is exaggerated in height, weight, and exotic look, while the male model continues to be six feet tall and weigh around 170 pounds. He and the size 40 suit seem eternal. The truth is that no matter how much the retail business and the designers for men would like to entice a new buying market, that market is very small.

If you are interested in working as a male model, avoid putting any money up front. Go directly to the largest city within your budget and have an interview at several agencies that you already have contacted. Open calls are great, too; but the competition scares some potential models off. There are scores of model competitors out there anyway, so the sooner you learn to deal with it all, the better for you.

You will need a look that the agent believes he or she can sell. Larger agencies have their own male models division. Peruse the men's fashion magazines, and you will quickly assess the looks currently in vogue. The want ads in large city newspapers as well as the Seventh Avenue papers to the trade will advertise for male models and will have job listings for fit models and some show and runway work. An agent is surely the best avenue to work in all the areas: catalog, photograph, print, TV, video, and even work for illustrators.

Television Models

The astronomical salaries paid for TV commercials finds actors and models battling it out. If the role does not call for speaking on the air, a model is usually acceptable, and a lot less expensive, to the client. Once an actor with a union affiliation is used, you are usually talking about a $20,000 payment. It is no mystery why any model would love to have one of these union cards. Anyone could be a television model, from the baby just able to sit to the aged who could do ads for elderly products. Famous people like sports figures and movie stars also do TV commercials, so the competition is the most frenzied here. Jobs are to be found in any trade paper or periodical, at modeling agencies, or through personal agents.

Television casting directors are inundated with thousands of applicants for every commercial. Auditions weed out the masses, and if you are lucky enough to get a callback, it's nearly a miracle. But someone will be chosen, and it could be you. There are ways to improve these odds, and the first step nowadays is to go to acting classes geared toward commercials and learn how to present yourself, as well as make it through the cattle-call auditions that can be so devastating.

There are tricks to every trade, and modeling for TV commercials is no different. If you're typecast, you'll click in a particular area, and the money is so stupendous that you can live on the income for one or two commercials for a year. Acting classes are for children as well as adults and are given in most big cities. Many supermodels are doing TV commercials for huge sums of money, as are little cherubs spitting out baby food for tidy double-digit thousands of dollars. Being a TV model could bring you that union card and the doubled salary for simply being seen and not heard.

Video Models

Millions of videos are made annually and entail professional modeling. Dozens of video machines are seen rolling in boutiques and department stores. The demonstrations could be anything from blowing up a mattress to cooking with innovative pots and pans.

Employed models discuss deployment of safety gear for airplanes, describe how to sell a particular product to a sales staff, and even do visual inventories like jewelry in a boutique. The possibilities are endless, and though pretty faces and hands are usually enough of a prerequisite to endorse these products, sometimes type characters are employed. Many men's products, such as men's perfumes, luggage, and clothing, are sold using male models. Although the runway shows that are presented live in Italy, Paris, and the United States are videotaped and shown to the masses, models are paid once, and there are no residuals like in TV.

Children demonstrating toys, high fashion models wearing full makeup for the client's company, and all the articles that you have ever seen or heard of potentially could be modeled on video.

A model may or may not have to speak. Acting always looks easy to those who have never tried it, as they assume models are simply being themselves. In truth, most individuals overact in this situation. A camera that captures you in an instant shot will surely give away all your insecure motions in a video. Watch the nervous eye motion or twitching hands of a person being videotaped. Calmness must be acquired. It is a dead giveaway that you don't exude confidence in either yourself or the product if your exclamations are punctuated with your hands moving faster than your mouth!

Video could work tremendously to your advantage as your résumé or as an example of your look as a model. Videos taken of you doing the unique things that you are qualified to incorporate into your modeling work could also be door openers. Agents and casting directors are bored to tears with the same old presentations, so that little extra eye-catching possible from a video may land you the job, and that's what this is all about—selling yourself first to the agent, then to the client.

Pay scale for video work depends solely on how big the client is and what he or she intends to do with the tape. It could mean as little as a few hundred dollars to double-digits in the thousands.

6

ATTRIBUTES NEEDED FOR MODELING

MANY ASPIRING MODELS make the mistake of thinking that attractive looks, good hair, and a long, lithe figure are all you need to make it in this business. To be sure, these attributes will help get you started, but to succeed, you will need much more.

Looks and Attitude

Hundreds of "workhorse" models and a handful of übermodels form the group that answers thousands of interviews set up by their agencies. You must sell yourself as the best model for the money and image to be made. Your agency merely makes the contact; it's up to you to land the client. Here is where personality and character count. It has become fashionable to depict a sullen, bored, or even a cynical expression in fashion shoots, but the attitude I am discussing here is one of professionalism only.

You must be hungry for the work and available for every go-see. Otherwise your agency will simply not try to get work for you. If you are easily discouraged by rejection, this is not a potential career. An optimistic attitude is paramount, and even if you've struck out for the last dozen go-sees, you'll have to appear fresh and ready to go every time a client interviews you.

Concentrate on your goal. If you are rejected on a go-see, never take it personally. If you never made the effort to get there, that's a different story. Your agency will keep trying for your probationary period just as long as you do. Even the most gorgeous person alive doesn't become a model instantly. Hard work derived from your innermost desire to be a model is the only way to make it.

A professional attitude toward yourself and your work is the next criterion. There are few other professions where you are so completely representing the marketable product (in this case you) in total. The client, your agency, the photographers, and even the stylists are silently observing. You need to be remembered for that next job and future jobs. It is of paramount importance that you leave a positive impression. This means being physically appealing, neat, immaculately clean, and having impeccable hair and nails. Many jobs are lost by models who are simply careless about personal care. When a model is not absolutely fastidious about cleanliness, an employer or client probably will not call that person for a job again.

You will want to own clothing that is recognizable as chic to those whom you are trying to impress. It's not a must that you have any identifying labels, but you must demonstrate your fashion awareness by wearing a generally "in" look. Observe other models' get-ups as they dress for go-sees. There is such a wide variance in self-sell modes that once you are a little more sure of your placement in the modeling agency, you are a bit freer to set differing looks for different jobs. Models—known and not so well established—can be seen on their way to jobs in New York City in everything from really ratty jeans to exquisite suits with a full complement of accessories. Models wear both ends of the fashion spectrum. Correct timing is the all-important key to when it's right to wear a certain look.

Physical Qualifications for High Fashion

Youth is paramount! High fashion models as young as 13 years of age are involved in career modeling. Their annual incomes rank among the highest salaries paid to any workers, including corporate executives, doctors, and attorneys. These very young girls are the beauties whose figures and faces are seen daily in publications and on television. Most of them are between the ages of perhaps 11 to 23. The really great high fashion model can stretch her career into her middle to late 20s, if she is very lucky. That is truly an unusual phenomenon, though, so the earlier you start, the better your chances are at making a career in this field.

The second qualification is that your height must be somewhere between five feet ten inches and six feet four. A really stunning beauty at five feet eight and a half inches could get by. The idea here is proportionate height with very slender limbs. So, if you are extremely fine-boned though shorter, you might still have a chance at high fashion work.

Weight is critical. You cannot weigh more than 115 pounds, and that would be on the tallest frame. Most of the models weigh around 110 to 115. Your weight has to stay consistent. This is accomplished by sticking to a highly restricted diet and by exercising.

The weight must be distributed proportionately over your frame. You must not have any bulges or even any visible bumps. Long and slender is the guide. Arms, legs, torso, and neck should be as lean as the proverbial racehorse. The bust is usually not larger than a C cup, but you could look into lingerie work if you are larger. Long, lanky, and nicely shaped legs are critical. Much of fashion depends on the height of the model and how the garment looks on the over-tall frame. The desired spot to carry the extra height is in the lower leg, not the torso or neck.

You must have a very photogenic face. This usually means straight features that are rather small. If you want to do runway work exclusively, you need not worry about being photogenic, but most models in the high fashion category combine all the areas possible to round out their careers, as well as their incomes. If you have some snapshots that look pretty bad, don't assume that you do not photograph well. It may be that all you need is a good professional photographer who will take the time to work with you. Few models photograph the way they really look. The camera can lie, and it's not a sure bet which way. Sometimes an incredible beauty looks almost ugly and vice versa.

Facial features can make a tremendous difference not only in your potential income but also in your total life as a model. The right combination of attractive eyes, alignment of nose, and alluring mouth is the difference between an average model and a million-dollar one.

Honestly assess what you see in the mirror. Makeup does help tremendously, but the bottom line basics are the aforementioned, plus no visible marks. If you have any scars, beauty marks, heavy freckles, or real variance in structure, they could count against you. Some freckles are considered to be very much in vogue, particularly in cases where the model is endowed with gorgeous red hair and golden or blue to green eyes.

Changing your physical attributes through plastic surgery is possible but advisable only if you are genuinely unhappy with part of your face—perhaps a small scar or mark. Modeling can be extremely fickle. What is "in" today could be as unpopular next month as the flu. Many times a model has been advised to have rhinoplasty, only to have a worse nose afterward or to discover that the original is now what is in style. Noses with bumps in the bridge, bushy eyebrows, slightly crooked smiles, irregular jaw lines, and ill-matched eyes are just a few of the trendy flaws that come and go in fashion work. Don't outguess the agents; what you consider an imperfection, they may be able to turn into a desirable characteristic.

Hair, teeth, and skin must be healthy, attractive, and vibrant. An all-around complement of appealing good looks is critical.

High fashion designers often seek out a certain "look" for their collections, a look that is instantly recognizable for their particular lines or collections. If you look at the fashion spreads, you will be able to see at a glance what style each designer develops. Some are enchanted with the classic beauty—fair hair and skin, light eyes, small tipped-up nose, and a generally English countryside appearance. Other designers prefer sultry brunettes to carry off the look of their collections. It is the complete impression of the coloring and facial expression of the high fashion model that is sought after for much live and photographic work.

The modeling agencies actually specialize in these various looks, and the largest agencies are able to supply everything from cute to sultry-looking models, depending on the client's needs. Newer models often try to develop a single look that they will be known for. Others are as wide-ranging in their look as a chameleon; you would really not believe that it could be the same person from page to page in a layout. Clever makeup, hairstyles, and clothing can and do create totally different impressions on the public's eye.

Varied looks that you will be required to create are affected by the costume, makeup, scenery, and mood you communicate through facial and body expressions. The cleverest models are good at mime; they can represent an action, character, mood, or feeling by imitation. Some articles of clothing lend themselves to a certain feeling on the part of the model. Imagination is critical, as there are often situations in which you are handed an item and are expected to wing it.

Easy movement is an enormous asset for the would-be model, as there isn't an easy way to learn the actions needed by the fashion world without a little innate grace and skillful emulation. Rhythm does not come easily to everyone, so the earlier that you become engaged in some kind of dance, sports, or music, the easier the art of moving well and with confidence will develop. If you have poise and self-assurance, moving like a high fashion model will be simple enough to learn. But if you have to start from the very beginning even to have ease of movement, you could be in trouble. As a young adult, poor carriage and stilted motions are a giveaway that you are really ill at ease, and this is a profession in which your basic job is to convey absolute self confidence.

The winning combination of desire, agility, great looks, height, slenderness, poise, facial beauty, proportionate figure, and youth is to be in possession of the right physical characteristics for a high fashion model. There are, of course, emotional and professional characteristics required as well.

Qualifications for All Models

Physical good health is paramount for modeling. The stress can be intense, the hours brutal, the travel wearing, and the weather trying for outdoor work. If you don't feel in top-notch shape, you're simply not going to last as long as you're required to, and exhaustion will cost everyone from your agency to the client.

Discipline is rigid for every model, children included. You must keep a consistent weight, build, and all-around "look." Your diet and exercise regimen must be strictly followed, and eight hours of sleep is critical for you to look and perform well.

Patience is a virtue you will need every time you have an interview, a go-see, or a session. Sometimes there are delays and hitches that make you want to scream. Keep calm as hysterics will make you instantly unpopular, and the others who can hold up under pressure will be the ones asked for return engagements. There is nothing worse than helping to make a bad situation a disaster, so try to remain cool while others lose their tempers. You'll be remembered and rewarded.

Enthusiasm makes the really great models. Sprightly young models are the mainstay of the business. They promote everything from foods to bobby pins with an effervescent quality that often appears to be genuine. Agents confirm that the person with the greatest charm, sparkle, and passion competes successfully with the greater natural beauty who lacks fire.

You must be able to take rejection as a daily diet without getting depressed. Every time you are sent on a go-see, the chances are that you only "may" get that job. As many as 15 people compete for each callback. You must keep a permanently optimistic view toward your career and yourself. This is the hardest part for many models, because rejection does make you feel discouraged. You have to keep trying and trying and trying. That seventh or eighth go-see just may be the clincher.

You need an endless ability to take criticism and work with it. You may be asked or even rudely told to do something like hold a very difficult pose. For all of your serious endeavors, it may not work. After agonizing for some time, the tempers begin to flare. You, as the model, are the target, and you simply have to keep trying to get it right. Criticizing is the only way some photographers are able to elicit the best shots, and if you're not an instantaneous "natural" (and about one in a million is "at home" in front of a camera, with photographer and stylists all demanding things of the model at once), then you have to give 1,000 percent every time you are asked to do a job. The cooperation of everyone is really visible in the final product.

Keep yourself organized with being fully prepared for every job promptly, enthusiastically, and professionally. Never be late to a go-see or an actual job. That is an unforgivable transgression. It keeps an entire group of people (who are getting paid) waiting, and you may never see another job through your agency again. If you are genuinely ill or there is a real crisis, you are expected to call your agency at the earliest moment so that the fewest people will be inconvenienced by the change in schedule.

You will not be able to have a full social life. When all of your friends are ready to start the evening's activities, you will be bowing out for an early night's sleep. When you are expected to look sensational at six in the morning, that means showing up looking rested and fresh, not haggard and with bags under your eyes. The only models who can get by with a normal social calendar are the television subjects for cold remedy and sleeping tablet commercials. Modeling is a difficult and highly disciplined way of life. Before choosing it, you should weigh the sacrifices against the rewards.

Qualifications for Male Models

Male modeling has never shared the spotlight in the same way as female modeling. A few years ago, the major work for the male model was work as a backup to the high fashion model or catalog work. The field has expanded so much that most modeling agencies have opened sections for the men only. The criterion is still the size 40 regular suit. There is a little variation in either direction. The main thing that the agencies are looking for in the male model is a really appealing face and slender body. The current look ranges from clean-cut collegiate to unshaven ruggedness.

The photogenic requirement is critical here, as that is the basic bread-and-butter area for men. Runway modeling is not needed as much for men, and though you might not need to be photogenic for that specific job, most runway work using male models is being videotaped. There is so little work for the male model that does not involve photography that he should not seriously consider a career in the field unless the camera is kind to him.

Agencies are looking for men between six feet and six feet two inches tall who lend themselves to the "look" that the agencies represent. A pseudotough look is currently in vogue.

Unusual facial features are most in demand. Look through men's fashion magazines and keep an eye on newspaper photographs of the current popular male models to get an idea of the needed features, haircuts, bone structures, and coloring.

Pretty teeth, sparkling or sensual eyes, and a fairly straight nose are required. Smaller features are the most fashionable-looking.

That lovely combination of perfect proportion in facial features and slender, tall body are the winning criteria for the male model.

Black and exotic male models are needed in all of the various areas of modeling. The ages of male models are more widespread than those of the females. A man in the field could last from his teens through his forties, as long as he maintains his good looks and his slender frame.

Qualifications for Child Models

Children are used in modeling for catalogs, television, and print ads. Child models are required to be very well-behaved and cooperative. Although you cannot expect adult behavior, absolute compliance is critical since they are working and are being paid for such. Child models must be unique, charming, appealing, cute, or pretty. They must be a perfect size. They must be photogenic, and they must want to work. It's not enough that they have all of the potential, unless they themselves desire to model.

The pay scale is enough to make any parent consider the prospects, but the child is the one who will be doing the sitting, so make sure that he or she really wants to work. If you have a child who you think might make a good model, send snapshots to an agency in your area, and they will get back to you if they are interested. Be sure to include a letter telling the child's statistics: clothing and shoe sizes, age, hair and eye coloring (if shots are black-and-white), height and weight, and any unusual talents.

Qualifications for Television Models

Anyone from newborns to seniors could be a television model. That covers the entire gamut of physical characteristics. The most often-used models are young, pretty women who promote products. Unlike the high fashion model, whose criteria we discussed earlier, these women could be anywhere from petite to Amazon in structure, and the men could have any look from the innocent little boy to the grumpy insomniac. The variations are endless.

There are two distinct parts of television modeling. You must be extroverted, determined, and self-assured to do the modeling, but you must also be capable of speaking for the medium if you're going to be doing the talking as well. You'll want to take lessons if you can't make the second half of the criteria, as the models who talk are the ones who get paid doubly. There is no such thing as being a wrong type for TV work; it's merely a matter of waiting until the demand for your look comes along. Certain people who are very talented appear time and again in commercials. They develop different characters for every ad. These models are often professional actors who not only have the advantage of possessing a look but also have the ability to be chameleon-like. If you are seriously considering TV work, try to do a little acting, and then contact a local agency to see what kind of headshot it requires; include it with your résumé at your interview.

7

Breaking into Modeling

A YOUNG MODEL hopeful is very fortunate if she has a mentor in her mother or a friend who knows the ropes in the modeling world. Inside information smoothes the way in a profession that can be potentially unpleasant or even risky. Youth and ambition and beauty are a combination that could make you easy prey to the many unscrupulous persons waiting to take advantage of you. This profession is particularly rife with pitfalls, especially in a large fast city. Where beautiful and very young girls are treated as commodities, it is often difficult to keep the path clear of hazards.

Look for the modeling agency with the most pristine reputation for safeguarding its models. The agency that takes precautions and carefully selects its clients is the agency that will safeguard you. Compare last year's *Yellow Pages* to this year's to see how quickly an agency can fail. Few modeling agencies last very long. Only a handful of seasoned modeling agencies continue to exist after five years' time.

Are You Model Material?

With all the constant press about modeling, it is easier to grasp your own potential if you can be a little subjective. If you live in an area far from major cities, you will have to rely on your own hunches and try to establish yourself as being attractive in the public eye. It is difficult without having the advantage of the professional's experience to judge, but you generally know if you might have the potential. That is the starting point.

If you've already been noticed by local photographers or been considered good-looking by others all your life, you are probably at least attractive. The only way to know what that might mean for you as a model is to proceed in the general direction of public affirmation of your physical attributes. Popularity must not be confused with possible modeling qualifications.

You will need some exposure to get a handle on public response to your ability to model. The tinier the geographical area, the harder it will be to gain this kind of exposure, but there are ways to expand this limitation. Contact local modeling schools and make an effort to write or e-mail agencies in nearby cities. You may want to enter local beauty contests and visit department stores and malls, leaving your name and photo (with your statistics and phone number). If a model is needed for a promotion, and you were clever enough to have left all the needed information, you will probably be the first chosen. It's happened more often than one would suppose that a "break" was prepared ahead of time by an aspirant, and luck did the rest. There is too much competition for these jobs for you to sit back and wait for them to come to you.

Suppose you are doing all right in a medium-sized city as a model. You may be perfectly happy there, and though the money is not earthshaking, you could make a decent living ($20,000 to $30,000) with runway work, promotional work, photographic work, and local television work. You are in demand and available full-time. If you are totally dependent upon your modeling wages, make certain to have a nest egg to tide you over, as modeling is often affected by fickle trends.

As a high fashion model hopeful, you will have to make your way to New York City, Los Angeles, or Chicago. Two smaller cities with moderate amounts of work to offer would be Atlanta and Cleveland in the east, and San Francisco and Dallas in the west. You may want to give these cities a try before you feel confident enough to approach the capitals of modeling. Any positive experience under your belt will be an added plus in your climb up the ladder in a modeling career.

The Beauty Contest

Young women by the thousands have entered beauty pageants in the hope of being discovered as models, starlets, and eventual celebrities. So much chance for media coverage comes with these contests that even if you are only a local winner, you could get quite a bit of mileage out of the publicity. There are also the added incentives of prizes and possible scholarships and contracts. It can be a surprisingly good stepping-stone.

Keen-eyed agents focus on the many contests that occur annually. Many an ignored contestant has become a top model, partly because beauty pageants are geared toward a much meatier body than fashion modeling and partly because most beauty contestants do not come across well in personal appearances, which is critical to the product promotions involved.

A few wannabes make a career of vying annually for places in beauty pageants. As an exercise in persistence goes, it is similar to the attitude that you'll need to have for modeling. If you really want to get into modeling, there are hundreds of model searches and beauty contests available to you. Start by looking online and reading magazines geared to the teenage market, and carefully select those contests that offer modeling jobs as prizes. There are many such contests, but the entry fees may be costly and the wardrobe another out-of-pocket expense. Some contests are so costly that sponsors are available, and you will have to investigate which ones will promote you the best toward your modeling goal. A local pageant may give you the experience that will help you get to the top in a bigger one, or you may want to try for the nationals right away.

A major drawback in the two largest contests (Miss America and Miss Universe) is the age requirement for entering. If you are young and set on a high fashion career, you may do better to give the smaller contests your attention, as many are geared to teenagers exclusively. Youth being the marketable item that it is, you may be wasting precious time by holding out for bigger stakes.

Some well-known beauty contests are given in the following list. It is best for you to e-mail each directly for information regarding the time, place, entry fees, and rules. Study the regulations and be aware of what they can do to help your career get started.

Miss Teen America Pageant
missteenamerica.com

Miss Ohio Teen USA
http://ohio.missusa.com/2-top.html

Miss Canada International
bconnex.net

National Miss America Coed Pageants
gocoed.com/main.shtml

America's Next Top Model
upn.com

Miss Alabama
missalabama.com

Miss World
missworld.org

Miss America Pageant
missamerica.org/competition/stateinfo.asp

Miss Ohio USA
missohio.com

Experience is critical as competition must be overcome in a way that you come out on top looking like you were just the best choice, not clawing tooth and nail to push yourself to the forefront. Everything has been tried, from researching the judges' backgrounds (to better prepare answers that would please their interests), to extensive plastic surgery (in the hope of being just what the judges are looking for). You'll do best by sticking with what you already have. Beauty contests are judged by human beings whose ideas of beauty vary widely. You could spend your entire life rearranging yourself to suit someone else's likes or expectations.

The recent nationally televised America's Next Top Model contest has garnered as many as five million viewers! This is a litmus test of the obsession that Americans have with beauty, contests, and modeling. The prize that attracted the hundreds of young women competitors is a year-long contract with a well-know New York City modeling agency. Twelve girls chosen from varied backgrounds and states come together to vie in the modeling world of emotional and fashion savvy and physical beauty portrayed in their photographs. The very green girls are developing before the nation's eyes as they try to get a grip on the actual life of a highly visual model. A polished professional is a must as thousands of dollars are spent on one commercial shoot. The girls must rise to the occasion and emote well, move well, and try daring feats to beat out their competitors.

Being a model is hard work, but we have glamorized the work to the point of luxurious celebrity due to the enormous salaries that can be made. The crash course in dealing with the competition and the critics is a gladiatorial event for the viewing public. We see the various girls and their specific fortes, what they lack, and what will be the winning package. It's a definite lesson for any would-be model. There are many options made available to these girls, and it is an interesting stepping-stone even for those who are disqualified. It's a cold-water, in-your-face introduction to just how brutally competitive the world of modeling really is. Each contestant is expected to display innate ability for fashion sense. This in itself is very telling, as few individuals are born with a sense of good taste but must acquire it through experience. These young women are tried and found wanting in different arenas, yet they display amazing poise in others.

The international search for Super Model of the World takes place annually throughout the world. To enter, contact the Ford agency in New York City. Its e-mail address can be found under the listings of agencies and schools in the back of this book. The agency will want to know your name, address, telephone number, date of birth, measurements, height, and weight. You will also need to enclose two snapshots or larger photographs: one head shot, one body shot. They need not be professional shots, and either black and white or color is acceptable.

Heading for the Big Agencies

You may want to approach the big agencies in New York or Los Angeles, where the largest amounts of money can be made. These agencies have open calls if you are nearby or you may mail (don't e-mail) your photographs to them to test the waters.

You might write or call to make an appointment with an interviewer. Agencies will want you to bring photographs so that the interviewer can see how photogenic you are. If you only have bad shots of yourself and you realize that they are awful, don't take them to an agent. The scrutinizing eye of the agent will tell whether you should invest in any shots. They might not be interested at all, and then you would be wasting your money and time. On the other hand, if you have good photographs of your face and full body, you will certainly want to show them to the agent. The agent will be looking at how well your figure and bone structure come across in a photograph.

The interviewers' keen eye is really critical in delineation of potential models. Their experience in what to look for can save you many hours of indecision. If you are just what that particular agency needs, you may happily end your search. If not, you must make another and another appointment until you have exhausted all of the agencies, large and small, that you would consider working for.

Give yourself a fair chance to get into an agency. However, after several months and some polishing of your whole look, if you are still pounding the sidewalks, start to think of another profession. The experts really do know, and there's very little that can be done to change the current selling look.

Breaking into Television Modeling

Some models are already working as photographic models when they make their first television commercial. They are guided by their agents, prepared for the audition, and know what to expect. Auditions can be pretty awful and are particularly noted for destroying egos. Of course, if you do land the part, you can feel really elated.

Arrive at the audition site at the scheduled time, check in with the receptionist, and then wait, nervously sizing up the competition. You will have brought your résumé and your head shot, which you will leave for the casting director to review or merely to remind him or her of who you were.

You will be introduced to other models who may be sharing this commercial with you. You will also be given your script and told the general story line of your little scenario. You may have a speaking part. If you do speak, you will have to memorize your lines as well as the cues and directions.

Having gotten this far, you are ready to go in front of the cameras. Things seldom go as planned. You may find yourself doing not one but as many as a dozen or more takes. If there are more people involved in the commercial, it could take quite a while just to coordinate everyone. Trying to make each take seem fresh and natural is easier said than done. Take number one may be stiff, but by the time you get to take number fifteen, exhaustion will have overcome stiffness.

If you develop the knack of television commercials, the thousands of dollars plus residuals paid will more than compensate for the boredom, anxiety, cattle-call degradation, and myriad takes.

If you don't land that first commercial, try again. If you believe that your hair is your best asset, try out for all the endless hair accessories, hair dryers, shampoos, rinses, dyes, clippers, pins, gels, curling irons, hair pieces, treatments, medications, highlighters, curlers, home permanents, and even stylists' commercials. Hairdressers' competitions have helped some models later obtain a hair commercial. Several known models got started with just such a TV commercial.

Unions strictly protect their people who perform in commercials, monitoring pay scale, time allowed to work, and where and when work can be done. When you try for your first commercial, you will not need to worry about unions; you are permitted a few "free" commercials before you must join a union (or unions). Your union sets a uniform pay scale that is higher than that of the person off the street. All ages of people are included in these codes. Your agent can advise you as to which unions to join and where and how to pay your annual dues.

There are two unions that you may need to join if you intend to do extensive work in television commercials: AFTRA (American Federation of Television and Radio Artists) and SAG (Screen Actors Guild).

There are rules as to which union coverage you will have to have. Lacking an agent, you must be responsible for your own protection. That means inquiring and applying for these union memberships as needed.

Your résumé is very important if you are planning to audition for television commercials. It must give all your critical personal statistics in a particular style or layout. Clever arrangement of the information, or adding an artistic touch, may help you catch the employer's eye. The most important thing is to remember that your résumé's function is to include all of the pertinent data; it also should be brief. The first section must include your name, address, and cell phone number (or that of your answering service, manager, or agent).

The next section should include your social security number and your union associations and membership numbers.

The following section should include your physical data: height, weight, hair color, eye color, and your general look or type. Include the age range that you could honestly portray. Your clothing sizes should be listed: for a suit, shirt, shoe, hat, and gloves if you are a man; and for a hat, dress, shoe, glove, undergarments, and swimwear if you are a woman. Most women are more detailed in the department of measurements. You may want to be explicit as to bust, waist, and hip measurements.

You will be promoting your vocal abilities (and talking in any commercial doubles your pay scale) in auditions and subsequently in commercials. Mention the level of your voice (tenor, for example) and list any movies or commercials you've done. Mention any live theater productions and the parts you acted. Give all the correct information about each theatrical production, including where and when it was performed.

If someone of renown coached you, list him or her clearly under the headings "Professional Training" or "Special Training." Also indicate any dance training, fencing, competitive sports, or any other type of movement instruction that could indicate agility or skilled grace. Mention any kind of unusual talent or skill—like skydiving, scuba diving, windsurfing, sailing, skiing, diving, ice-skating, horseback riding, pizza tossing, whistling.

The ability to speak any foreign languages should be noted as well as your nationality and native tongue if it is not simply North American. Even variations in United States accents can make or break your chances at the job.

Your photograph, which is so important, should show a lively image with projection. You should spend a good bit of time working on this. An employer will want to see how you will come across as a warm, believable, likable person. This is not an easy request of one sample photograph.

After spending much time in front of a photographer who specializes in head shots for television commercial hopefuls, you may come up with one or even two passable shots. Try to get another professional opinion about which shots to use. The expense of these head shots will be $500 to $1,000, depending on your choice of photographer and how many prints you decide to make. This can be a rather large investment if you are doing many auditions, and you leave the photograph with attached résumé with the casting directors of each. But this photograph can be the reminder that could and often has secured a future or even a different job than the one you tried for.

Can Modeling School Help You?

Modeling schools were first established in the thirties and forties when professional modeling began to rise with product-association sales. In the smaller cities, you can find many a school-agency that introduces the totally green model to the basics of the business and gets your first work as your agent.

Modeling schools do not offer the promise of any success. Their job is merely to show a little of the inner workings of the profession. As far as becoming a model with or without a future, it is merely a chance endeavor on your part. It would be unfair to assume that the modeling school can make you into a model any more than any school can produce a graduate with a guarantee of success. Carefully investigate the benefits of the modeling school before you enroll. It could be a complete waste of money and time if the agency of your choice wants to provide its own instruction, leads, and guidance.

Depending on your actual limitations as far as modeling jobs, you may find it very beneficial to take a modeling school course that is given in conjunction with local contacts and known work. A word of caution: many scams are now growing around the modeling industry, particularly involving the schools and false promises. So check out any institution with your Better Business Bureau before you enroll.

Seeing how you appear on film and video can give you insight into your potential future in the varied areas of modeling. Mock-ups of actual "shows" will prepare you for work with commentators, as timing is an essential in this work. Every modeling situation will be different, but the more aware you are of what may occur, the more confident you may feel.

There are modeling schools in every major city where you could inquire about the courses given, the time allotted, and the cost. Some of the schools are strictly charm instruction and will simply give the student a little polish. In really rural areas, self-improvement courses are valuable simply as an introduction to basic fashion.

The reason for attending any school is to learn something that you did not know before. Hundreds of people do have all the raw qualities needed. For people who already have great self-assurance and all the needed physical attributes, attending modeling school would be superfluous.

These schools give modeling instruction, charm classes, pageant preparatory courses, and general self-improvement instruction. The modeling course should include posture, carriage, and walk; diet, exercise, and figure control; nail care; skin care; hair care and styling; wardrobe coordination and fashion; and etiquette and social graces. Classes should also familiarize the young person with all the terminology and some of the equipment needed for the modeling trade.

In the New York City area, the tuition for between 45 and 60 hours of instruction would be about $1,300 to $2,000. Techniques for the various areas of work are stressed. In a very rural area, it is often through this one channel that the completely naive youngster gets started. So even if the outlay of the tuition is a bit of a gamble as far as your guaranteed return (no one can promise you of even one modeling job from your schooling): it can also be the leg up that will get you into the real arena.

In larger cities like Atlanta, Cleveland, San Francisco, and Boston, modeling schools are more visible. Some of these schools have associated agencies that help students find work.

In New York City, a modeling school should be looked into as carefully as any other institution. Merely the fact that it bears a New York City address does not guarantee that it is good. The classes may be spread over as many as nine months or be as concentrated as one month. They are for both men and women and should include the basic knowledge needed to start with any agency. Help is given on how to handle your interviews at agencies, what pictures might be needed, and how to compile a résumé.

Photographs

Agents observe that it takes several months for models to relax enough to be able to really present themselves. There is something inhibiting about finding yourself a few feet away from that critical little eye of the camera's lens.

Most photographers try to elicit the right mood from you with music, or subtleties in voice, directions, and atmosphere. Some of the most interesting shoots are taken "on location," where the product or the fashions would most likely be used. Usually, you get to film outside. It's not everybody's idea of fun—the wind, rain, heat, or freezing cold can put a damper on things.

Feeling inhibited must be overcome before you will be able to do your best work in front of the camera. Many agencies in New York City that hire you will see to your development. It could mean an internship in Europe with many photographers. These photographers will teach you how to move, how to "freeze," and how to develop your own special attitude and "look" for the camera. They are known for being very patient and will work with you until they get the correct look on film. The pictures are often quite beautiful and become part of the models' portfolios when they return to continue their careers.

One way to acquire great photographs is to ask other models which photographers took theirs. You can then call the photographer and ask if he or she is testing. If tests are arranged, the model takes the film and pays for processing. The photographer gets to pick from the slides. Both are responsible for their own printing. This benefits both parties, as both need shots for their portfolios. It is a very good way to make contact with as many good photographers as possible. The photographer is often the one who makes recommendations to the client, and that's a plus for you. If you are a good model for the photographer's work, he or she will be able to promote you.

Portfolio

Your portfolio is the most important representation of your modeling work. Every time you have an appointment for a potential job, you must drop off your portfolio. The client then studies all of the types of photographs that you have displayed and decides whether you would be the perfect model for the work that will be photographed.

Portfolio photographs currently cost between $1,200 and $3,000 in New York City. Check with the agencies of your choice if you are planning on taking professional shots to interviews. Printing is costly and you should think ahead, or you may find yourself spending more money than you thought possible.

Most photographs using models have a credit (the photographer's name), so if you see photographs in a style to your liking, you may want to contact that studio. For television modeling, you have to have photographs going in. Head shots for this specialized type of modeling should depict you at your warmest and friendliest; your fashion photographs would be unsuitable.

Expect to pay $500 upward for a head shot for television commercials. This would be an 8 × 10 in black and white that you would leave at all the go-sees, accompanied by your résumé.

Many times when the selection is to be made, it is only your photograph in a two-foot-deep heap of them that reminds the director who was even there. You can see how critical good photographs are to your potential work. You may not be selected for the original job you were seeking, but that photograph left on file sometimes gets you another totally unrelated job. Get noticed, and then be the one and only one who's remembered. Casting directors see thousands of hopefuls every day, and many are pretty much the same or could feasibly do the same commercial, so they are impressed with the uniqueness that you can project in the two minutes flat that you'll be viewed initially.

Beginning Expenses

If you are moving to New York City or Los Angeles, you will have to have a large nest egg to tide you over, unless you are planning on working at some other job while you try to break into modeling. The rent alone will probably be much more than you are accustomed to paying. Many models share their apartments with one or more other models.

Food will be the next most expensive item in your budget. Food costs in New York City have doubled in the past few years. It used to be possible to save money by cooking at home; now food is so expensive that it is often just as reasonable to go to a neighborhood restaurant.

Transportation costs are rising steadily, too. New York City buses and subways are now $2.00 per ride, and taxis are about $5.00 a mile in the city, considering the heavy traffic.

Medical and dental expenses should be anticipated. You won't be able to fly home when your filling comes out in an untimely crunch. A filling could cost about $300. New York City is really not a place to be caught without medical insurance coverage.

Add all of the above figures together, plus an allotment for personal items, entertainment, household items, telephone ($150 deposit), and gas and electricity, and you will have an idea of what it could cost you to live.

Add the cost of the photographs that you may initially need, the cost of your portfolio case itself ($150), your makeup (which will be extensive if you are a woman), clothing, and any sports gear that you might require. Nobody ever said that New York City was an inexpensive city to live in or that modeling was an inexpensive profession to get into. It is a game to juggle all of the figures; eventually you'll come up with your own solutions on how and where to save pennies.

Upsides and Downsides of Modeling

Competition in modeling has brought the profession to a new level, both for the astounding money to be earned and the ages of the models. Females as young as 13 are completely on their own in cities like New York, Paris, and Los Angeles. Some of the more reputable agencies have addressed this issue by offering housing dormitory-style to some of their novice models. Too often a young girl on her own finds trouble in the form of unscrupulous agents, photographers, and others near the industry who prey on the weakness of the wannabe model and will try to take advantage of the situation. Burned-out teenage girls are endless victims of the missed brass ring on the carousel of modeling. Some of the young male models are destroyed as well, but their numbers are many times fewer.

The successful females who have risen to the top are not without their own problems. The big money is the opiate of the model; hooked and trying to find meaning in a totally illusionary world, she is addicted. If you can discipline yourself to use the earnings from modeling to further yourself in a more in-depth career, it is often more rewarding. If celebrity and big money are ends in themselves, you may find happiness to be elusive. There is also the reality that youth will vanish and that you will need a second career sooner or later.

No matter how glamorous the life of the professional model looks to the observer, it is still a very disciplined job. Modeling has been promoted as a luxurious style of celebrity with an aura of ease, fun, excitement, and instant prestige. It has truly been the path to super riches and status for a few super models. It is often that promise of success and fame that entices the young to seek modeling careers. Hearing from the models themselves gives a bit of insight into the realities of the daily down-to-earth work. Here are some of the day-to-day pros and cons of the trade:

The Advantages

- "The money is terrific. Nobody would think of paying me the kind of money that I make as a model, so I plan to stick with it as long as I can."
- "The best part is getting to go 'on location' because it's usually somewhere pretty exotic, and it was out of the question that I'd ever get to see any of these places before I got to be a model. I've been to Italy and Japan, and Greece is a possibility."

- "Just having been a model for as long as I have been was an experience that no one could take away from me. It was kind of an education in itself."
- "I just happened to be lucky. My girlfriend and I started out together, and even though she is really a beauty naturally, I'm the bigger success because I wanted it so much more."
- "You get a lot of self-confidence from working as a model. Between the rejection and the praise it can be a little much, but it keeps you going if your head is where it should be. I know that I'm a good model and that it's hard work. It gives me self-satisfaction."

The Disadvantages

- "You always have to be 'up,' and even after days of being told that you're not the person for that particular job, you can't let yourself feel dejected. It's all part of the game."
- "You never know how long a client will want you to represent the product. It's a real day-to-day risk."
- "I can never eat whatever I'd like. I have to think of the deprivation tomorrow if I have pizza tonight."
- "I'm really torn between continuing my modeling and getting a degree that I know I'll need very soon. The money is great right now, but I'll have to be behind all my friends if I put off my college until later."
- "It's hard to be in a profession where you know that you'll be a has-been by the time you're 22."
- "Go-sees are really nerve-racking. It would be great to get all of your work through recommendation."
- "New York is a hard market to crack. You have to be a strong person. It's a vicious business, and you have to sift through it. You have to see it for what it is."

- "The fact that you never know that you will definitely have work worries me. I want to know that I'll be able to meet my bills. So many of us are out there now."
- "The worst part for me is seeing how great the more seasoned models' books are. It'll take me a long time to get my photographs up there."
- "The discipline is really rigid. I wish that I could take a break from my diet, exercise program, and daily schedule, but if I'm not visible, there are just so many other girls who are dying for the work that I can't relax!"
- "My boyfriend accuses me of being self-centered. I know that modeling is a 24-hour job, and if I don't watch out for my future jobs, nobody else will. We fight a lot about how much time my work takes me away from our relationship, but I really want to model, and I hope that we can stay together, too."
- "It's hard to put up with some of the temperaments of the designers, stylists, and even some of the other models, but personality conflicts can be a problem in any line of work."

A Few Helpful Hints

You must be as well prepared prior to your attempted launch into the modeling world as is physically possible. So get in top condition.

Your smile is a paramount introduction to you—not only for cosmetic reasons, but because bad teeth tell the world that you don't think enough of yourself to take care of them. The male model is primarily noted for his teeth (and his eyes). Men have to have a great smile to sell the product. Women models have to have pretty teeth as part of the whole picture.

Makeup is a critical factor for all women models. Applying makeup is an art. When you do a fashion shoot, a makeup artist or stylist does your face. This can be as time-consuming as two hours or more. If you are doing catalog and other similar types of work, you will have to do your own makeup and do it well.

There are many tricks of the trade. Some of these can be picked up at places where makeup artists work on you, advise you as they go along, and show you how to bring out your best features. You are expected to buy makeup, but you also will pay for the makeup artists' work. Shading and highlighting are two of the most important things that you have to learn.

Your fingernails have to be perfectly manicured. That means they should be really scrubbed, with no visible cuticle, and either coated with clear polish or buffed to a soft shine. Your nails are right out there, and there is no way to hide a lack of care on your part. Become adept with the emery board, and keep both hands looking neat. Once you've started to make an income as a model, you'll want to head straight to the manicurist and the pedicurist once a week.

Leg waxing is critical for a model and is done on an as-you-need-it basis. Most women go to the salon at least once every six weeks, but if you are averse to all this time consumption, you may want to consider removing hair from your bikini line, legs, upper lip, underarms, and eyebrows by electrolysis. In the long run it could save you money and time.

Develop your fashion sense as soon as possible. Exposure to art classes, sewing courses, and familiarization with costumes in museums and libraries are all helpful. You are not often expected to create your ensembles for actual modeling work, but your own fashion sense will be valuable in your presentation of the clothing in front of the camera and in your presentation of yourself.

Dance classes, acting and speech lessons, and voice instruction may be very helpful if you are aiming toward television work as part of your modeling profession. Any plays having a possible part for you should be given serious preparation and an audition.

Experience before an audience—choral singing, plays, variety shows, beauty pageants, and even attending social functions—can be helpful in giving you that critical self-confidence. Poise is gained by experience. Though modeling can only be done well by the truly experienced model, your efforts to feel at ease in front of lots of people can aid you tremendously when you are asked to "perform" before the cameras.

8

THE BUSINESS OF MODELING

NO ONE WHO knows the business has ever said that modeling is easy. The work itself, as we have seen, can be arduous. Therefore, it will help you to know a little bit about the business aspects of modeling as you start to feel your way into this career.

Salaries

There are 95,000 models currently working in the United States. The two reasons given most often why persons want to become models are to be rich, famous, or both. Celebrity models have sped up to übermodel status. It is no longer enough to make the million-dollar salaries for those at the top of this field. Recognition and idol-worship have become the great salary boosters. It now costs clients stupendous amounts to have their products represented by a recognizably famous model. The cosmetic companies with their immense profitability are the big contracts to the models. Celebrity models are more often associated with makeup and fragrances than with any other products. Models who represent or are exclusive to one makeup or fragrance company may not represent another. However, they can accept other types of modeling jobs and are not restricted solely to that one company.

Models can expect to earn commensurately with their locale and the advancement of client requests. Small-town models are often paid per job or a bit above minimum wage, while the more opportunity-filled big city can land you a salary of as much as $300,000 if you are working to capacity. The paycheck will reflect your rate of demand from a modest $15,000 to a pretty stunning bankroll of more than a quarter of a million dollars, and these females are often only 13 years old!

Runway work is usually paid at around $150 per hour and could run a bit more or less depending on the time of year, the actual promoters, the number of models needed, and the size of the return expected from that showing. If the show is a very lavish one and continues for an extended length of time, that will be taken into consideration and the pay could run as high as about $250 per hour. Runway and fashion shows do not always have cash remuneration in the smaller cities; the pay may be made in clothing or even in makeup.

There are also photographic jobs available in moderation, depending on the size of the city and its prominence in the local fashion world. For the department store's advertising in the local newspapers and brochures, you could expect to be paid about $75 per hour.

Agencies in rural areas have a set rate for which the model may be hired. That rate would apply to whatever job the model might be requested to do, from live promotional work (where he or she might otherwise only make the doubled minimum wage) to photographic work. The agency might ask 20 percent, for example. This seems quite fair in that the agency then looks for better-paying jobs and you have a chance at developing a reasonable income. The idea here is that you would like to be a model only and not have to subsidize your income forever with other work.

Local manufacturers sometimes hire models for their showrooms. Such work, though seasonal, pays about $40 to $50 per hour. The work is only available a few weeks during the year, so you could not consider making a living from it.

There is simply not enough income available from modeling in medium-sized cities for you to have a real career of it. Ultimately, to make a career in modeling, you have to move to Chicago, Dallas, New York City, or Los Angeles. The experience gleaned in a smaller town will have given you a bit of self-confidence and will hold you in good stead. You will learn that having done your homework in any size city is what forms the basis of professionalism.

Not long ago the top salaries for the fashion models in the middle-sized cities ranged from $10,000 to $16,000 a year. These were the best and the busiest models, and yet that was all the work that was available to them. Women in New York City who are just starting out with an agency are paid between $150 and $300 per hour depending on the kind of modeling. Male models in New York City have a starting pay of between $100 and $200 per hour depending on the agency. Some will and do pay up to $300 per hour.

The way to build up your hourly wage is by building up your popularity. Agencies push their top models; if you work your way up to that category, you could be making more than $400,000 in salary. A particular look comes in, and if you have that look, your agency will capitalize upon it quickly. Fashion can be quite fickle. While you have the in look, you will have to move fast.

Catalog Work

The area known for its bread-and-butter support of models is catalog work. You've seen hundreds of catalogs stuffing your mailbox, especially around Christmastime. The catalogs are distributed from department stores, mail-order houses, food importers, sporting goods merchandisers, toy manufacturers, travel packagers, and many more. The companies hire models to demonstrate their wares or beam unself-consciously in everything from silk underwear to million-dollar furs and diamond necklaces.

The more prestigious items will be modeled by the highest-paid models. Though the salary may start at $180 to $250 per hour in the bigger agencies, your potential is really unlimited, and there are catalog jobs that pay extremely well. If a model's fee is $500 per hour, and a client has that look in mind as the marketable face, that client knows what prestige a known model's face can bring to the product and its sales. It is popular to have a known rather than unknown face and figure—thus the constant search for new models who could become the coveted look of tomorrow. There is a similarity in the look of many of the known models, and though there is a professed trend to deviate from the tall-blond-and-leggy look, the demand from the clients still keeps them the highest on the want list.

The editorial rate for the high fashion models is generally pretty low. The current rate is around $150 per day starting pay. Editorial is modeling work that does not promote a product such as soap or toothpaste, thus the lower compensation. A model must do this kind of work in combination with commercial catalog work to survive. Generally speaking, any woman in high fashion could do catalog work, but most of the models that you see doing work in catalogs are not high fashion models.

You can tell by looking at the models if they are high fashion or not. Scan high-end publications for models with particular elegance and élan. Your eye will become accustomed to a certain polished look and demeanor. You won't be able to distinguish this by what they are promoting or what they are wearing, but by the stance, projection of attitude, and "feel" of the model.

The more projection the model has, the better the look of that person will be remembered, and that's what will make the hourly rate skyrocket.

You will want to do a mixture of both catalog work and fashion work. Although catalog is the bread and butter of modeling work, with a pay scale of $180 to $250 per hour, without fashion work you won't hold your own in the industry. You must have a good balance of these two types of work to remain a photographic model represented by an agency.

You are, of course, paid for your time while you are being made up, having your hair styled, and having the clothing fitted before a photographic session.

Runway Work and Fashion Shows

Pay will differ even if you are doing somewhat the same type of work. Runway work done in various hotels for business groups and some social functions is occasionally done by models just starting in the field, some fresh out of a modeling school. The models are offered this experience in exchange for photographs and are not remunerated in cash. The photographs and the experience itself are both very valuable to the inexperienced model.

Informal modeling in department stores in New York City is on a pay scale of about $100 to $150 per hour. These models are seen walking through the store in everything from expensive gowns to bathing suits. They are always exceedingly thin but not necessarily photogenic.

Big fashion shows could pay as little as $250 or as much as $500 per hour. The model is compensated at half that pay while being fitted. The fees can go much higher than the aforementioned rates. One Seventh Avenue showroom pays $300 per hour for runway work. It all depends on where it is in the world and where the show lies in the fashion season.

If you choose to work for a showroom on Seventh Avenue as a model, you will gain experience but not get paid a great deal. This is a weekly job with a weekly salary. Some models like the security of the nine-to-five job, but the difference in your potential salary is significant. The weekly salary would vary according to your experience and the type of garments required. Most of Seventh Avenue does not require a high fashion model, and there is work to be found there even if you are as short as five feet six inches. You need only be moderately attractive and pleasant in personality, as you deal directly with customers. You could be modeling any garment from junior sportswear to bathing suits. Current weekly salaries for the huge variety of Seventh Avenue models can be found in the want ads in the local papers.

Try to go to several interviews if you plan to work on Seventh Avenue or in the department stores. It will give you an idea where you will fit in best. Both are live modeling jobs, and both could potentially lead to other things. The main difference is the figure type required. The Seventh Avenue model could be the shorter, bustier woman. The department store model who shows women's clothing will have to be at least five feet eight inches or taller and weigh less than 120 pounds. Some Seventh Avenue models will have the high fashion prerequisites also. If this seems a bit confusing, it is because the garment district has very different needs in its models.

To get a clearer idea of who might be modeling on Seventh Avenue, wander through the endless sections of junior to large-size clothing in the stores. If a garment is sold, it was probably modeled for a buyer at some point. To narrow the field, read the specifications in the daily want ads that are calling for models for the garment section.

Women over five feet eight inches tall and weighing 150 to 200 pounds are much in demand. These women are needed by the market to model the clothing that most women now need. Not only are more women taller than ever, but they are proportionately filled out. These models can find work not only on Seventh Avenue, but also in photographic work to sell the large-size clothing. The salary level here potentially could be more than $200,000 per year. Everything from large-size swimming suits to evening gowns need to be modeled, so there are plenty of jobs available in this area. Not all agencies handle the large-size model, but you would definitely want to be handled by an agency to guarantee the highest income, unless you wanted to start in the garment district where you would be a weekly salaried employee.

New models just starting out should not expect to make anything for the first three months. After that the jobs should start coming in and the model should reasonably expect to have at least three jobs a week. By the beginning of the second year, you should be making at least $50,000, and from then on the sky is the limit. You will bring in just as much as you yourself are willing to work for. There are always appointments to go to. If you are enthusiastic and have the needed look, you'll be out there perhaps six or seven times every day on go-sees. No one who has worked as a model could ever call it anything but very hard work. The model who pushes constantly could certainly see a salary above $250,000.

Take all jobs with as much variety as possible to take advantage of your youth. Remember that this career cannot last past the age of 23, unless you are extremely lucky and your face shows no lines. So if you work extra hard every day and are certain that you want this so badly that you're willing to give your all, you're sure to make it.

With a good agency behind you, and the two of you cooperating on your career, you might just become one of the million-dollar models. You'll never know unless you get out there and explore the field. You have to start early. Right now is not too soon.

Modeling in Other Countries

Modeling abroad as a way of entering the field has its pros and cons. When you are signed by an agency, an apprenticeship (period of learning) in Europe to work with fashion, makeup, photographers, and methods of handling yourself and paraphernalia usually lasts about six months. At that time, most fashion models return to their agencies in the United States. If you should be lucky enough to land some paying work in Europe, you could find yourself working in England, Sweden, Denmark, Belgium, France, Holland, Germany, or Italy. If you decide to return to any of these countries at a later time, you will probably find enough modeling work to keep you happy while you enjoy Europe as well.

There are, of course, many "on location" jobs where an American model or several models are sent to work. These stays are not lengthy, and many models complain that they have been places but had so little time to sightsee that they don't know anything about where they were. At some point in your career, you may want to relocate. The money to be made in modeling is excellent worldwide.

Exclusive Contracts

Most models hope for an exclusive contract with a company whose product they are hired to represent in every type of media possible. The people who first come to mind are those women whose faces have been the sole (or almost sole) model for the huge cosmetic companies. Exclusivity means that the model will only be photographed in that company's cosmetics. This prohibiting act is very expensive for the client. By cutting off the model's other possible sources, the hiring company contracts her at a fee that must satisfy her and compensate for all the potential work that she might have been able to do. Exclusivity is so highly paid that most models are very desirous of such an arrangement. The best part of this type of contract is, of course, the security and the fame that come with being associated with some of the most prestigious products. Exclusive contracts have been known to reach three million dollars for a three-year contract, and every year these star jobs get even higher dollar fees.

Inexperienced Versus Experienced Models' Fees

The fees indicated in this chapter for the various types of modeling are all the bottom rates. As a model becomes better known and is more in demand, the agency will raise her or his fee. It works somewhat like the supply and demand in any business. The model's fees keep increasing and level off when the demand does. The demand could just stop altogether, so one has to be prepared for many eventualities.

The lucky and very rare model whose career takes flight instantaneously could make that million-dollar salary, or more. Only one lucky model in ten thousand will make it at all, and the ratio is even greater—much greater—for supermodels.

The models who are making such high yearly salaries are combining many forms of modeling—high fashion, runway, television, catalog, editorial work, videos, and even posters. The money to be made from all of these sources collectively is stupefying.

While the model has a look that is salable, the money must be made and quickly. Youth does not wait, and popularity can and does wane, so the clever model makes all the money possible during her halcyon days.

Agents, Agencies, and Managers

Fueled by the thousands of wannabes, the modeling agents have now assumed a defensive position. Inundated with frenzied requests and endless photographs, they are in the catbird seat and can dictate whom they will see.

Agencies have always needed rosters of varied models for the prospective clients to select from. It used to be most advantageous for models to look around at what each and every different agency could possibly offer them. Now it is all you can hope for if at least one agency takes a serious interest in you.

At one time it was possible to freelance by using small agencies, contacts, and referrals. Today, if you don't have an agency behind you, you're almost sure to get lost in the hordes.

The ideal would be to have an agency represent you that would send you to at least several go-sees per day. With the current status, many models could be the perfect one for the client, so it is just that much more difficult to become established.

Small agencies are able to push you a bit more but may not have the bigger clients, while the large and more established agencies have many more models to choose from who may take potential work from you. Also there are certain styles and characteristics of all the better-known agents. Often the youngsters sink or swim due to the mentoring relationship of their agents. Agencies have a vested interest, as you will be the one making the fees that keep the agency afloat. You pay them the normal 20 percent and the client pays them as well. So there are many reasons to have as good a representation as is possible.

You may be thrilled that an agency has agreed to take you, but if you feel that you are not being handled to your best advantage, you can always wait out your contract and then go on. In the past, some of the bigger models in particular have sought their own personal managers to guide their tremendous financial contracts. Agents, like all others, can be wonderful, or not so wonderful. Personal agents are only as good as the return they can get for the both of you.

Selecting the Right Agency for You

The drastic reversal in the agency's position has made it critical that you size up the situation and choose the best possible agent to go to first. Each agency specializes in a certain style. Familiarize yourself with the various models that agency represents. You will see the similarities in their overall look, and you must then judge where you think you fit in best.

Weigh the advantages and the disadvantages of the smaller versus the larger agency prior to calling for an appointment. A smaller agency would more than likely be able to get you more work, but its pay scale could be as low as half of what you could make at one of the bigger agencies. One tremendous advantage to working for smaller agencies is that they are more likely to mentor you if you are completely green; thus you will gain experience and become polished in the interim.

The bigger agency is in a better position to pay the larger fees to models. However, though you may be sent on nearly twice the number of go-sees as the smaller agency could send you on, the larger agency has more models for that same client to interview for the same job.

When you interview at the agency, let the interviewer do the talking. Listen carefully and answer all of the questions as concisely as you can. Most of the questions will be to establish your height and measurements and to get a reasonable understanding of what you expect from the modeling world and how you think that the agency will fit into the scheme of things.

Questions like "Why do you want to model?" and "Why do you think that you would be good at it?" are just two of the things they'll be likely to ask. Remember that they can be very personal, and you should be prepared to take personal questions in stride.

At your interview do not be modest, but do not brag either. Any extra talent that the agency may be able to promote for you is money in both your pockets. If you are a good athlete, dancer, skin diver, or even were in many serious dramatic productions, be sure to mention it at your interview.

No one can tell you beforehand if you will be hired by any agency; on the other hand, you may be offered a contract within minutes of your interview. Be prepared for both possibilities. You cannot take the lack of an offer as a personal rejection, as the interviewer may honestly believe that you might fit in better somewhere else, in which case to hire you would be a disservice to both of you.

If an interviewer sees no future in creating a business relationship, you must take it as a positive statement and simply look into another agency. It is less likely that you will have to go to more than one interview if you can correctly comprehend the types of models that each agency represents.

Having been just hired by an agency, you cannot even imagine how much it can guide your destiny. It is up to the agency to send you where you can potentially perform at your very best for both of you. You are in business together, and though it may be able to open some doors, your own caliber of work and self-sell will have to keep those doors open.

An agency will sign you only if it believes that the contract will be mutually beneficial. This means that the agency will do everything in its power to promote you, to get auditions and interviews lined up for you, and to make you into a more salable look. Therefore, it is of paramount importance that you and your agency be not only compatible, but also really honest and straightforward with one another.

Fees

Agencies must set your fees for the various types of work that you will be doing. They set up your go-sees, and it is up to you to give it all you've got—to get to the appointment on time looking great, make the right impression, and present your book and yourself as professionally as possible.

The agency is there to protect you. Once it has set your fees and you have done a job, the agency will bill the client and collect your fee. You are responsible to your agency for a percentage of your fee for services rendered. There are no set percentages, but you can expect to have your agent charge about 20 percent. Some agents charge per big contract. Be certain that these things are spelled out clearly in your contract.

The Agent's Job

The agency is your answering service, business manager, book-keeper, secretary, adviser, tutor, and even your guide as to weight reduction, hairstyle, makeup, and diet. The agency protects you from unscrupulous clients and unprofessional people with whom you may come in contact. A model does not have to accept a particular job if he or she does not wish to. The power of the agency can make it more difficult for less than legitimate contacts.

Agents see to the right model selection for go-sees. It is their business to comprehend what the client wants and what model will be dispatched. It behooves the agency to have very clever people in its employ for discretionary selection. If agents judge incorrectly, a model from another agency gets the job.

Once under contract, you have to be sent on many go-sees to get started. If you are working in a small, slower agency, you could see three to four clients a day. A larger agency might send you on as many as seven or eight go-sees a day.

You will have only a few months; then if you do not start to "move," the agency may lose interest in you. Those first weeks are the make-or-break probationary time, so you have to convey your uniqueness, charm, and effervescence in a hurry.

If you are planning to move to a large city to work for an agency, it will often help you find housing. Ask your agent about this possibility if you are going to have to relocate to work.

Agencies are divided into different divisions if they handle large numbers of men, women, children, and a variety of television jobs, runway work, and shows. There is so much complex work involved that it would be next to impossible to cope with the needs intelligently without having the various sections. Most models take advantage of as many kinds of work as their agency can offer them.

Many models feel that you are not taken as seriously if you try to freelance (work without being represented by any agent). A city like New York is so big that unless you have many personal contacts and know all the ropes, you are likely to find it nearly impossible to operate as a freelance model. The major benefit to being a freelance model is that you would not have any agency fees to consider in your budget. But if you cannot get any modeling jobs without the aid of the agents, then, of course, you have saved half of nothing.

Zed Cards

Most big agencies help defray expenses for your composites by supplying Zed cards. These are rather small cards with several photographs of you arranged in some sort of fashionable array. The composite is made of several of your selected photographs and is left with the client as your calling card when you have completed a go-see. This little card often gets you work at some future date, as the client can then just open a file and find you; though you may not have been perfect for the original job, you may be for subsequent ones.

Portfolios

Portfolios are notoriously expensive. The book itself could cost $1,000. One roll could easily run $50 to $100, and you'll need at least 10 to 12 different prints. By the time that you will have completed a good portfolio, it will have cost about $2,000. A good agency helps build up your portfolio through "testing" (they send you to the photographers, and in return you and the photographer will get prints) and spares you having to pay for the best photographers.

Agencies help you to select the photographs that are best for your portfolio. Their keen eye is honed through many years in the business, and its experience is financially valuable to both of you.

Control

Your agency has a great deal of control over whom you will or won't work with. Having a good agency behind you can literally make you, as opportunities are made available for you to work your way up the ladder. The agent sets up the critical connections, and you have to cement them. With a large amount of luck, pluck, and energy, you can make it in the modeling field. The hardest part is getting started. Now that you know that the agency has put its vote of confidence in you, the rest is up to you.

9

STARTING YOUR OWN MODELING AGENCY OR SCHOOL

MANY AN ENTREPRENEURIAL model has formed a new agency or school. Familiarity with the profession gave them the insight into its shortcomings and how to eliminate some of them in their own businesses. The combination of a past great model and a business partner is often seen. Business acumen is critical to the success of any endeavor, and you need only to look at the tremendous turnover of modeling agencies to see how precarious the business is.

Creating an Agency

Competition is your greatest concern in setting up your own agency. As models become more desired by clients so do agents desire to take their cut. You will need to look at all the potential snares and possible edge that you hold over established agencies in the area. If you plan to have several divisions within the agency, you will need a reasonable amount of space. If you intend to specialize, you can get by with as little as one room with a receptionist, secretary, booking agent, and you. Because of the intense competition, how you attract your clients and models will be your most challenging problem.

Make certain that your chosen location will have the aura of chic, as that is the product that you are selling. If your agency is too far from an "in" neighborhood, neither clients nor models will take you as being adept in your field. Organization is very important, too; you want to keep close track of your models and your clients.

As a model/agent entering the business world, you have to arm yourself with a completely different way of thinking. You will do well to take a few business courses and scan the general information in the course offerings from business schools. There are also advisory boards whose members are retired business executives. Their wisdom could guide you onto the right path without endless trial and error.

Financially, you will have to consider the rent, telephone, receptionist, bookkeeper, a secretary or two, advertising, cost of furnishings, salaries of employees, taxes, booking operators for your models and clients, and general office and business machines. Visit an agency or two comparable to the type and size of the one that you are planning. As a current (or past) model, you have a good idea of the inner workings of an agency, but if you've been working as much as most models, there are a lot of details that would have slipped by you. That was what you were paying your agent to do, to see to the smooth running of the agency so that you were free to do your end of the work.

The modeling business being what it is guarantees tough competition among modeling agencies for the advertisements. The money to be earned is so stupendous that every agency is vying for a larger and larger slice of the pie. If they weren't aggressive, there wouldn't be any jobs for you or them, and they'd be out looking for other work if they couldn't handle the struggle for power.

It is not really possible to know if you have the type of personality that can cope with all the wheeling and dealing, but it's certainly not a consideration to take lightly unless you are planning to have the one and only agency in an entire area.

Starting a Modeling School

A modeling school would be a serious undertaking due to stringent laws, competition, and potential students in that area. Depending on its location, a school may need certification from state boards and from local boards. To find out the requirements in your area, contact your state's capital for that information. A modeling school is also considered a business and thus has to pass certain standards according to the Bureau of Consumer Protection and the Better Business Bureau.

Judge whether the area in which you want to locate will support a school of this nature. In some areas, you might find a mere handful of students, which would necessitate your expanding the school to teaching other curriculum or expanding to include all age groups. The possibilities all should be carefully weighed before investing your time and money.

After you have tested the waters and found the area to be amenable to the idea of a charm or modeling school, select the location and amount of space accordingly. You may hope to get contracts for advertising from local merchants after you produce a few polished models who could work for them. This bit of confirmation might help you decide if expansion plans could be part of your near future.

Finances should be a major consideration. It may take quite a while to become profitable. Schools can be very successful, but expenses can also be high—rent payment, insurance, telephone bill, receptionist, advertising, textbooks, electric bill, rental for video equipment, cameras, makeup, faculty, and allotted amounts for guest lecturers to keep the instruction up-to-date. Fashion itself is only that if it is fresh and new.

Instructing is very different from modeling, of course. Patience is indispensable, and the desire to help someone else to learn and understand is the priority. If you think that you would enjoy teaching, volunteer before you take instruction courses. You may or may not want to actually instruct. There have been hundreds of masters in their own select fields who not only realized that they were miscast as instructors but also truly hated the teaching end of the professions that they adored as performers.

Give serious thought to the possibility of running a school. Its popularity may or may not be an integral part of the area in which you reside.

Potential Earnings

Small town modeling agencies could make around $20,000, while a modeling school could possibly do the same or better. A medium-sized city would have more people from which to draw both students and clients. For an agency to survive, there have to be both merchants and models from which the client can choose. The risks are greater, and so are the potential profits.

To give you an idea of how an agency makes its money, consider the following: an average model in a medium-sized city is currently making about $15,000 per year. The agency should have at least a few dozen models capable of this income. The agency collects about

20 percent of their job incomes as its fee. Given all the expenses of running the business of the agency, the money could be pretty tight. Certain areas of our country are still handling a large amount of the entire modeling industry. New York City, Los Angeles, Chicago, Dallas, and a handful of the middle-sized cities are the main hubs. These centers seem to be the better business spots for starting an agency or a school of modeling, although you also encounter greater competition from other existing schools and agencies by locating there.

If you were to own a franchised modeling school, the income would depend greatly on your ability to attract students. There would obviously be better locations than others. These schools are scattered over the 50 states, as required by the population centers. The lowest-paying ownerships or franchises would run around $25,000 per annum, and the largest incomes in owning your own modeling agency would be well up in the millions.

Owning a modeling agency is not everybody's forte. The stress is incredible and the competition deadly. You may want to look into possible related work other than owning or managing a modeling facility, but you are your own best judge. There are very successful agents out there. You may have it in you to be one also.

10

FUTURE JOB OUTLOOK FOR COSMETOLOGISTS AND MODELS

THIS CHAPTER WILL give you an idea of what to expect in terms of outlook and salary as you embark on a career as a cosmetologist or model in the exciting world of fashion and beauty.

Male Models in Demand

Male modeling continues to expand and develop. Most major modeling agencies have opened divisions for their male models due to the expanded market. Men are now working as runway models for shows and videos, doing print and live work, and edging into the fashion world still dominated by the female models.

Emergence of the male as an admired figure for his looks alone is a new trend, and the male modeling world increasingly capitalizes on the idea. Underwear for men has become very status-oriented, and as a result many male models are being hired for their beautiful physiques.

High-end men's clothing markets have created thousands of modeling spots. It would not be unusual for a male model to make more than $150,000 per year after he started to become established. If he "takes off," his salary could well be over the $200,000 mark. Men model the gamut from photographic work to television commercials. They do extremely well at paycheck time and are able to maintain their careers for many years.

Male models are most frequently used for catalog work. This can be their bread and butter for decades if they are preferred by one client and remain attractive. Very little of men's clothing changes style from year to year, so their work is just not as innovative.

Some modeling schools accept male models-to-be at age 13 and upward. These schools know that the male model is mostly interested in television commercials and thus stress that particular area of instruction for men. Preparation for the television commercial is best learned through acting classes sometimes taught in modeling school. The other area where the male model does well is in the print area. The school could be helpful in preparing him for the camera, makeup, and stance.

A male model could be hired by an agency from about $150 to $300 per hour as his starting rate. If he becomes popular, his rate increases.

The Future of Modeling for Women

Modeling is assuredly a female-dominated world. It is at the top as far as salary to be made, and salaries continue to increase. Female models tend to take advantage of this unique position and continually flood the agencies with new wannabes. They use their image to glean as many options as possible while youth is on their side.

While increases are shown in the number of female models registered, the actual employment of male models has not grown much on an annual basis.

Many female models are branching out into the entire spectrum of modeling possibilities to make as much money as is available while they are employable in the field. The newest market for the female model is that of video, which is an ever-increasing market. From high fashion to the promo model, much more exposure via video is seen than ever before.

An area that has opened up for the teenage female model is high fashion, with extremely young women showing women's couture (fashion). These young girls are taking over a market that had been solely reserved for women at least 10 years older. Young women of 11 to 13 are the representatives of the high fashion market, and salaries they command fall in the highest ranges. There are contracts offered and signed in the hundreds of thousands for the right look in the preteen years. This trend started years ago and continues to grow. Major agencies are hiring younger and younger girls who previously would have been employed by an agency for children's modeling.

Salary rates per hour vary widely depending upon the client and type of job. Catalog work pays from $12.50 to $5,000 per hour depending on the circumstances. Children average around $125 per hour for catalog work. Many female models are now started at pay scales of $1,500 per day, and the scale rises with demand for the model.

Female models have more choices today than ever. The salary per hour has been rising and the opportunity to work in hundreds of different locations has also expanded the viable market. Ambitious young women are working in many major cities in Europe,

Scandinavia, Australia, and Japan, as well as in other large cities in the United States.

The Future of Television Modeling

Television modeling continues to burgeon beyond all predictions for making money. There are endless possibilities for variety in this medium. A male model who portrays a he-man, wimp, pizza-tosser, or skydiver can make large amounts from television commercials.

For the female models, anything from high fashion to the hands only is possible. All areas for women are soaring. There is no shortage of work in television, but there is endless competition. When a hand model can make $535 a day, you can see why everybody wants a slice of the most well-paying pie.

Male models are making a much more obvious dent in television commercials, as their clothing goes more and more into designer fashions. The men's cosmetic industry is taking off, as is the entire array of leisure items from home computers to sporting gear.

Child models are also doing extremely well, from tiny babies to teenagers. Their field encompasses the major portion of the toy market (which is sizable), children's clothing and shoes, medicines for children, and a myriad of other possibilities. In fact, the market is so lucrative that many child models are surpassing their counterparts in the adult modeling world. It's an old adage that everyone loves puppies and babies, and it has paid its weight in gold in the television commercial world. As a case in point, there is a five-year-old child model who is a celebrity and is interviewed frequently on talk shows!

The area of television commercials has so expanded that many major modeling agencies that handled basically photographic models have now added separate television divisions to their ranks. Many models used to have the modeling agency do the booking for everything except television commercials; now they are able to have their modeling agent handle the whole market. Some agents and managers who do not run modeling agencies handle television commercial models.

Television has a very solid future and promises many jobs for models of both sexes and the widest variety of ages. The television industry runs on the money of sponsors, and they are in continual need of models to demonstrate their products.

Because of the exorbitantly high pay scale, famous models and actors do battle for the big TV commercials. The biggest names in show business are out there as your stiffest competition for that high-paying commercial for cars or cell phones.

Billions of dollars are spent annually on commercials for television. That indicates the strength behind the market for the continued need for thousands of television models.

Outlook for Cosmetologists

In the United States Department of Labor's *Occupational Outlook Handbook*, the most current statistics available offer the following projections for opportunities in cosmetology.

There will be 239,000 new jobs by 2005 for those in the cosmetology industry, approximately 18,384 new openings per year. An estimated 218,000 of the new positions will be filled by hairdressers alone. The total numbers currently of barbers and cosmetologists combined are 790,000. Of these numbers 711,000 are cosmetologists. The job outlook is noted as being greater than the average for other employment right through the year 2005. Cosmetologists and manicurists account for the major increases as the barbers decline slightly. Many barbers have discovered that they must do hairstyling to stay competitive.

The projection for earnings in this field is between $20,000 and $35,000 a year, depending on the area of the United States. The number of clientele and the amount of your tips have a direct impact on your earnings.

The projected increase then will continue at the rate of approximately $3,000 to $7,000 per annum, depending on the aforementioned factors of geographic location, number of customers, and, of course, the cost of the cosmetological procedures.

In 2000, there were about 711,000 cosmetologists employed in the United States. They worked in beauty shops, unisex shops, department stores, hospitals, and hotels. In 1994, statistics showed that 671,400 persons were employed as cosmetologists. At that time, the projected growth was excellent. It is obvious that this particular field is expanding greatly, and if it continues at the indicated pace, there will be an abundance of jobs available.

The overall picture for the future of cosmetology is an exceptionally bright one. Many people complete cosmetology schooling, take the state boards, become licensed operators, and then do not seek full-time employment. The statistics only tell us how many persons hold cosmetology licenses and do not go into detail as to how often, or even if, many of these operators join in the workforce. There will always be openings for qualified hairstylists. The demand is continuing and growing. All the cosmetology services need to be filled to capacity, and there are jobs continually becoming available.

Salaries

Average earnings for a cosmetologist who is just starting out amount to between $12,280 and $17,660 per year. The projected highest

10 percent will make about $33,220 as soon as they have an established clientele. Remember that this is an average figure and that there are cities where the salary could be much higher and less-populated areas where it could be lower. Tips are notably larger in the bigger cities and easily could amount to one-third of the wage.

Salaries and commissions normally are negotiated before an operator accepts a position with a salon. Much depends upon the experience and the following that the operator is bringing into the salon. If a large following will accompany the operator, it is not in his or her best interest to settle for a straight salary. Obviously the clientele will continue to increase, and the operator should benefit as well as the salon owner.

Commission arrangements are normally 40 to 50 percent of the total for the operator. Only if an operator had no following and was just starting out would he or she consider a minimum guaranteed salary. Specialists and stylists with experience earned salaries around $25,000 a year in the mid- and late 1990s. Those same operators are probably earning more than $32,000 today plus tips.

Cosmetological Associations, Modeling Agencies, and Information Sources

THE FOLLOWING ORGANIZATIONS will be able to provide you with the information you need to help you make your beauty or modeling career plans a reality.

State Boards of Cosmetology

All states (including the District of Columbia and Puerto Rico) have a state cosmetology board that sets requirements for schools, salons, and individual cosmetologists. The rules vary from state to state. If you want to know the rules for a particular state, you should e-mail the state board for this information. The telephone number of the state boards is listed below only if it does not have a Web page.

Alabama Board of Cosmetology
aboc.state.al.us

Alaska Barbers and Hairdressers
dced.state.ak.us/occ

Arizona Board of Cosmetology
cosmetology.state.az.us

Arkansas State Board of Cosmetology
state.ar.us/cos

California Department of Consumer Affairs, Bureau of Barbering
　　and Cosmetology
dca.ca.gov/barber

Colorado Board of Barbers and Cosmetologists
dora.state.co.us/barbers_cosmetologists

Connecticut Department of Public Health
dph.state.ct.us

Delaware State Board of Cosmetology and Barbering
professionallicensing.state.de.us

District of Columbia Cosmetology and Barbering
http://dcra.washingtondc.gov

Florida State Board of Cosmetology
myflorida.com

Georgia State Board of Cosmetology
sos.state.ga.us

Hawaii Board of Barbering and Cosmetology
state.hi.us/dcca/pvl

Idaho State Board of Cosmetology
www2.state.id.us

Illinois Department of Professional Regulation
dpr.state.il.us

Indiana State Board of Cosmetology Examiners
in.gcv/pla

Iowa Cosmetology Board of Examiners
Department of Public Health/Professional Licensure
idph.state.ia.us/licensure

Kansas Board of Cosmetology
ink.org/public/kboc

Kentucky State Board of Hairdressers and Cosmetologists
(502) 584-4262

Louisiana State Board of Cosmetology
state.la.us

Maine Board of Barbering and Cosmetology
maineprofessionalreg.org

Maryland Board of Cosmetologists
dllr.state.md.us/occprf/cos.html

Massachusetts Board of Cosmetology
state.ma.us/reg/boards/hd

Michigan Department of Consumer and Industry
michigan.gov/cis

Minnesota Department of Commerce, License Division
commerce.state.mn.us

Mississippi State Board of Cosmetology
E-mail: nluckett@msbc.state.ms.us

Missouri State Board of Cosmetology
ecodev.state.mo.us/pr

Montana Board of Cosmetologists
discoveringmontana.com/dli/cos

Nebraska State Board of Cosmetology
hhs.state.ne.us/lis/lis.asp

Nevada State Board of Cosmetology
state.nv.us/cosmetology

New Hampshire Board of Cosmetology
(603) 271-3608

New Jersey Board of Cosmetology and Hairstyling
(973) 504-6400

New Mexico Board of Barbers and Cosmetologists
(505) 476-7110

New York Department of State, Division of Licensing Services
dos.state.ny.us

North Carolina Board of Cosmetology
cosmetology.state.nc.us

North Dakota State Board of Cosmetology
E-mail: cosmo@gcentral.com

Ohio State Board of Cosmetology
state.oh.us/cos

Oklahoma Board of Cosmetology
state.ok.us

Oregon Board of Cosmetology Health Licensing Office
hlo.state.or.us

Pennsylvania State Board of Cosmetology
dos.state.pa.us

Puerto Rico Board of Examiners of Beauty Specialists
estado.gobierno.pr

Rhode Island State Board of Hairdressing
health.state.ri.us

South Carolina Board of Cosmetology
llr.state.sc.us

South Dakota Cosmetology Commission
E-mail: cosmetology@state.sd.us

Tennessee State Board of Cosmetology
state.tn.us/commerce/cosmetology/index.html

Texas Cosmetology Commission
txcc.state.tx.us

Utah Board of Cosmetology
dopl.utah.gov

Vermont Office of Professional Regulation/Board of Barbers
and Cosmetologists
sec.state.vt.us

Virginia Board of Cosmetology
state.va.us/dpor

Washington Board of Cosmetologists, Barbers, Manicurists,
and Estheticians
wa.gov/dol/bpd/cosfront.htm

West Virginia Board of Barbers and Cosmetologists
state.wv.us/wvbc

Wisconsin Barbering and Cosmetology Examining Board
drl.state.wi.us

Wyoming State Board of Cosmetology
E-mail: barbern@statewy.us

Cosmetological Associations

American Association of Cosmetology Schools
15825 N. 71st St., Ste. 100
Scottsdale, AZ 85254-1521
beautyschools.org

American Electrology Association
106 Oakridge Rd.
Trumbull, CT 06611
http://electrology.com

Cosmetology Advancement Foundation
208 E. 51st St.
New York, NY 10022
cosmetology.org

International Guild of Professional Electrologists
803 N. Main St., Ste. A
High Point, NC 27262
igpe.org

National Accrediting Commission of Cosmetology Arts
  and Sciences
4401 Ford Ave., Ste.1300
Alexandria, VA 22302-1432
naccas.org

National Barber Career Center
3839 White Plains Rd.
Bronx, NY 10467

National Beauty Career Center
3839 White Plains Rd.
Bronx, NY 10467

National Beauty Culturist League
25 Logan Circle NW
Washington, DC 20005
nbcl.org

National Commission for Electrologist Certification
96 Westminster Rd.
West Hempstead, NY 11552
scmhr.org/ncec.htm

National Cosmetology Association
3510 Olive St.
St. Louis, MO 63103
salonprofessionals.org

The Society for Clinical and Medical Hair Removal
7600 Terrace Ave., Ste. #203
Middleton, WI 53562
scmhr.org

World International Nail and Beauty Association
1221 N. Lake View
Anaheim, CA 92807

Partial List of Modeling Agencies and Schools in the United States and Canada

Alabama

Real People Models and Talent, Inc.
2829 Second Ave. S
Birmingham, AL 35233

Arizona

Beverly Hills Modeling Agency
9100 N. Central Ave.
Phoenix, AZ 85020

Model and Talent Management
7426 E. Stetson Dr.
Scottsdale, AZ 85251

California

Artist Management Agency
835 Fifth Ave.
San Diego, CA 92101

Campbells Models and Talent
1617 N. El Centro Ave.
Los Angeles, CA 90028

Look Model Agency
166 Geary St.
San Francisco, CA 94108
lookmodelagency.com

Models
7083 Hollywood Blvd.
Los Angeles, CA 90028

Next Model Management
8447 Wilshire Blvd.
Beverly Hills, CA 90211
nextmodels.com

Top Models and Talent
870 Market St., Ste. 1076
San Francisco, CA 94102

Colorado

John Robert Powers Modeling
4305 Beverly St.
Colorado Springs, CO 80918
johnrobertpowers.com

Connecticut

Faces Model Management
209 Bruce Ave.
Greenwich, CT 06830

Tom's Casting
523 E. Putnam Ave.
Greenwich, CT 06830

Florida

Benz Model and Talent Agency
15908 Eagle River Way
Tampa, FL 33624
benzmodelandtalent.com

Ford Models
311 Lincoln Rd.
Miami Beach, FL 33139
fordmodels.com

International Models, Inc.
8415 Coral Way
Miami, FL 33155

Look Model and Talent Agency
3532 N. Ocean Blvd.
Fort Lauderdale, FL 33308

Models Scout, Inc.
651 Rugby St.
Orlando, FL 32804

Georgia

Arlene Wilson Model Management
887 W. Marietta Street NW
Atlanta, GA 30318
arlenewilson.com

Convention Models and Talent
2996 Grandview Ave. NE
Atlanta, GA 30305
cmtagency.com

Hawaii

Kathy Muller Talent and Modeling
   619 Kapahulu
   Honolulu, HI 96815
   kathymuller.com

Premier Models and Talent Agency
   1441 Kapiolani Blvd.
   Honolulu, HI 96814
   susanpagemodeling.com

Illinois

Elite Model Management
   212 W. Superior St.
   Chicago, IL 60610
   elitechicago.com

Ford Models, Inc.
   641 W. Lake St.
   Chicago, IL 60661
   fordmodels.com

Shirley Hamilton, Inc.
   333 E. Ontario St.
   Chicago, IL 60611
   shirleyhamilton.com

Indiana

American Models International Modeling Agency
   2500 Harmony Way
   Evansville, IN 47720

TP Modeling
    5843 Haverford Ave.
    Indianapolis, IN 46220

Iowa

Corell Modeling and Talent
    1970 Grand Ave., #35
    West Des Moines, IA 50265
    corelltalent.com

Talent Model Placement
    222 Third Ave.
    Cedar Rapids, IA 52401
    tmpshowcase.com

Kansas

Focus Model Management
    155 N. Market
    Wichita, KS 67202

Kentucky

Alix Adams Model School and Agency
    9813 Merioneth Dr.
    Louisville, KY 40299

Louisiana

About Faces Model and Talent Management
    929 Julia St.
    New Orleans, LA 70113

Fame Agency
 4518 Magazine St.
 New Orleans, LA 70115
 fameagency.com

Maryland

Nova Models, Inc.
 2120 N. Charles St.
 Baltimore, MD 21218
 http://novamodelsinc.micronpcweb.com

Massachusetts

Barbizon School of Modeling
 607 Boylston St.
 Boston, MA 02116
 modelingschools.com

Maggie, Inc.
 35 Newbury St.
 Boston, MA 02116

The Model's Group
 374 Congress St.
 Boston, MA 02210

Michigan

About Faces Productions
 26500 Northwestern Hwy.
 Southfield, MI 48034

Class Modeling/Talent Agency
   2722 E. Michigan
   Lansing, MI 48912

Jabo Model Management
   211 Logan St. SW
   Grand Rapids, MI 49503
   jabomm.com

New York

Boss Models, Inc.
   1 Gansevoort St.
   New York, NY 10013

Click Model Management
   129 W. 27th St.
   New York, NY 10011
   clickmodel.com

Elite Model Management Corp.
   111 E. 22nd St.
   New York, NY 10010
   elitemodel.com

Faces Model Management
   16 Evans St.
   Buffalo, NY 14221

Ford Models, Inc.
   142 Greene St.
   New York, NY 10012
   fordmodels.com

Gilla Roos, Ltd.
16 W. 22nd St.
New York, NY 10010
gillaroos.com

IMG Models
22 E. 71st St.
New York, NY 10021

Next Management
23 Watts St.
New York, NY 10013
nextmodels.com

Wilhelmina Models, Inc.
300 Park Ave. S
New York, NY 10010
wilhelmina.com

North Carolina

Avanti Model and Talent
1401 Diggs Dr.
Raleigh, NC 27603

Face National Talent
1230 Morehead St.
Charlotte, NC 20217

Ohio

Extreme Model and Talent Management
6412 Sharon Woods Blvd.
Columbus, OH 43229

Jo Goenner Talent
2299 Miamisburg, Centerville Rd.
Dayton, OH 45459

Mélange
3130 Mayfield Rd.
Cleveland Heights, OH 44118

Model and Talent Management Agency
256 Easton Town Center
Columbus, OH 43201

Pro Model and Talent Management Agency
3296 W. Market St.
Akron, OH 44333

Taxi Model Management
1300 W. 78th
Cleveland, OH 44102

Pennsylvania

Expressions Modeling and Talent Agency
720 Church St.
Philadelphia, PA 91908

Reinhard Model and Talent Agency
2021 Arch St.
Philadelphia, PA 19103
reinhardagency.com

Van Enterprises
908 Perry Hwy.
Pittsburgh, PA 15229

Rhode Island

Character Kids
  1645 Warwick Ave.
  Warwick, RI 02889

Model Club, Inc.
  2695 Main St.
  Providence, RI 02903
  modelclubinc.com

South Carolina

Millie Lewis International
  389 Johnnie Dodds Blvd., Ste. 101
  Mt. Pleasant, SC 29464
  http://millielewis.com

Oasis Promotion
  9400 Two Notch Rd.
  West Columbia, SC 29223

Tennessee

Barbizon
  105 Lee Pkwy. W
  Chattanooga, TN 37402

Barbizon School of Modeling
  6711 Kingston Pike
  Knoxville, TN 37919
  modelingschools.com

Model and Talent Management
5028 Park Ave.
Memphis, TN 38117

Texas

Bravo
2620 Fountain View Dr.
Houston, TX 77057

Dallas Model Group
12700 Hillcrest Rd.
Dallas, TX 75230

First Class Models
5090 Richmond NE
Houston, TX 77056

K. Hall Models and Talent
1195 Angelina St.
Austin, TX 78702

Maxxam Modeling Studios
7711 Gulf Freeway
Houston, TX 77017

Model Forms Agency
5319 Gulfport Dr.
El Paso, TX 79924

Tricia Holderman Agency
5210 McKinney Ave.
Dallas, TX 75205

Virginia

Barone and Co.
5599 Seminary Rd.
Falls Church, VA 22041

Washington

Heffner Model Management
1601 Fifth Ave., #2301
Seattle, WA 98101

Seattle Models Guild
1809 Seventh Ave.
Seattle, WA 98101
smgmodels.com

Washington, DC

The Artist Agency
3333 K St. NW
Washington, DC 20007

Washington Models, Inc.
1133 Thirteenth St. NW
Washington, DC 20005

Canada

Agence Girafe, Inc.
381 Notre Dame Ouest
Montreal, QC H2Y 1V2

Agence de Mannequins Cosmos
   1117 Saint Catherine Rue Ouest 803
   Montreal, QC H3B 1H9

Blast Models
   615 Yonge St.
   Toronto, ON M4Y 1Z3

Reinhart-Perkins Modeling and Talent Agency
   2120 Queen E
   Toronto, ON M4L 1J1

ABOUT THE AUTHOR

SUSAN WOOD GEARHART is a professional model, dancer, and free-lance writer and editor. She graduated from City University of New York and attended Hiram College, Juilliard School of Music, and the Preibar Academy in Berlin, Germany. She has worked as a professional model since her teens and has covered the field from artist's model to television to runway work. She has modeled for a wide variety of products, from cosmetics to bathing suits, and has made a career of freelance, agency, part-time, and full-time jobs.